ATTITUDE

 S0-BJJ-940

ATTITUDE

commonsense defense
for women

Lisa
Sliwa

**with
Keith Elliot Greenberg**

**and photographs
by Jill LeVine**

**Crown Publishers, Inc.
New York**

Publisher's Note:

This book contains instructions for self-
defense techniques for women. Careful
attention should be given to the specific
instructions, and the suggestions and warnings
regarding their implementation.

Copyright © 1986 by Lisa Sliwa

All rights reserved. No part of this book may be
reproduced or transmitted in any form or by any means,
electronic or mechanical, including photocopying, recording,
or by any information storage and retrieval system,
without permission in writing from the publisher.

Published by Crown Publishers, Inc., 225 Park Avenue South, New
York, New York 10003 and represented in Canada by the Canadian
MANDA Group

CROWN is a trademark of Crown Publishers, Inc.

Manufactured in the United States of America

Library of Congress Cataloging-in-Publication Data

Sliwa, Lisa.
   Attitude: commonsense defense for women.

   1. Women—Crimes against—Prevention.   2. Women—
Attitudes.   3. Safety education.   I. Title.
HV6250.4.W65S55   1986   362.8'8   86-6270

ISBN 0-517-56187-5

10 9 8 7 6 5 4 3 2 1

First Edition

This book is dedicated to my mother,
Gloria De Michiel Evers,
my beloved mother-in-law,
Frances Sliwa,
and to the many unsung heroines
of their generation whose everyday actions
have shown me why life is
worth fighting for.

It is also dedicated to Mildred
Glover, Annie Rogers, and all the
mothers of the missing and murdered
children of Atlanta.

CONTENTS

I WASN'T BORN ON THE SUBWAY

The first thing I heard when I came to was the sound of my belt being ripped open. I opened my eyes and saw an angry man kneeling over me, his pants down, exposed and ready to rape me. He seemed confident that he could take me without any kind of struggle.

For an eternal instant, I was in a panic that far outweighed my intense physical pain. I could barely move anything. Behind my attacker, two men kept watch while he shouted obscenities at me: "This will teach you a lesson! I'll stick you good! I'll show you, bitch, who's the toughest! You think you're so bad, let's see your karate now!"

I was on the fourth floor of an enormous abandoned building on New York's Lower East Side. At one time, it had been a thriving community center, but years of neglect had turned it into a decomposing shell. As part of a Guardian Angels project, we were trying to make the building into a headquarters and service center for the city's homeless. I had just sent two Guardian Angels out to get building supplies and was working in a small, dusty office next to what had once been a gym. The three men had walked across the gym floor nonchalantly. They were white and well groomed—which made them stand out in this neighborhood—but I still had no reason to be fearful.

"Can I help you?" I asked.

"We're looking for you, Sliwa," one of the men said threateningly.

"Can I help you?" I repeated, more sternly.

"We have a message for you."

I thought about running, but I wasn't sure how far I'd get. I decided to stand my ground.

The three thugs had the whole scenario planned out. I was pushed into the office, put into a choke hold and beaten. The men taunted me with each blow: "Tough chick! Where's your big, bad husband now?"

Now, with the beating completed, my attacker had me down on the floor, ready to put the frosting on the cake. What really upset me was that all my martial arts training seemed ineffective. My karate 11 background had made me think of myself as almost invincible. Now, I was too weak to employ any of the techniques I knew. It had all happened so fast.

I realized I had no time to feel sorry for myself. I made the decision that this man was not going to rape me. I knew I had one shot at an escape, and it had to be right. My attitude was, I'm going to live, and nobody is going to rape me.

Fueled by the tremendous anger my decision evoked, I grabbed my attacker's genitals, pulled hard and squeezed. Fearing I might not have the strength to do any damage, I forced my head up and bit his thigh. Then I started to scream for help.

The noise and the pain shocked the guy on top of me. For a moment he stopped. Then, one of the others said, "Tony, this isn't what we came here for."

"I'm going to get you," Tony snarled, rising. "If I don't get you now, I'll get you later." And they ran.

I crawled out of the office, across the rotting wooden gym floor, threw myself down four flights of concrete-and-metal steps and pushed out the front door onto Second Avenue. I don't remember who spotted me first. I just remember being put in a police car and taken to Cabrini Medical Center.

What that day showed me, in very graphic terms, was that it isn't your physical strength that's going to help you get through a violent situation. It's your attitude. My commitment to survival saved me. This book is about finding the same commitment within yourself.

Some people think that I was born on the subway, but I actually grew up in a very affluent suburb of Chicago, where the worst crime you could commit was wearing the same dress to a party as another girl. I was the perfect suburban princess—honor student, cheerleader and highly decorated Girl Scout.

Besides being one of the most conservative communities in the United States, my hometown of Hinsdale, Illinois, remains one of the safest. In a 1985 *USA Today* survey, it was rated the fourth safest community in the nation. When I was a child, nobody worried about having a bicycle stolen or—in those days before the 1981 Atlanta child murders heightened everyone's awareness to the grim realities of child abduction—being kidnapped.

Italian on my mother's side and pure white bread on my father's, I was fortunate to be part of an ideal American family. My father, John, was an engineer, and my late mother, Gloria, was a registered nurse with a bachelor of arts degree in English—which made her slightly different from the housewives of her generation.

I'm the oldest of six children. After me, there's Christopher, a systems analyst for a Minneapolis investment company; Nina, a development officer in a Seattle hospital; Jimi, who recently graduated from Syracuse University with an architecture degree; Tedd, a basketball star and student at Harvard; and Charcy, still in high school and living with my father and his second wife, Mary, in Ridgewood, New Jersey.

The atmosphere in our home while I was growing up was wonderful: full of love and encouragement from my mom and dad for whatever we wanted to do—as long as it wasn't watching TV. Our house was always the center of activity for the neighborhood, with kids running in and out, phones ringing off the wall, blaring music and nonstop teasing and clowning around.

My parents, like many others, made a lot of sacrifices to give us the best possible life. Despite the pressures on them and their total lack of privacy in a household filled with rambunctious children, they somehow managed to give each of us special attention and find time to get involved with our activities. It wasn't all the lessons and privileges they gave us that made them great parents, it was their nonstop love and support.

My "baby" brothers were athletic and certainly contributed to my early tomboyish tendencies. We'd play touch football in the yard, wrestle on the living room carpet and have plain old-fashioned fights all over the house. We did a great job of getting on my tolerant parents' nerves. Even though my brothers are younger, by the time they were in junior high school they towered over me.

I always had girlfriends, but after school I usually played with the boys. Their games were more physical and exciting. My favorites were kick the can, various derivatives of tackle football and pom-pom-pullaway, which consisted of two teams trying to knock each other down. But I was still very much a girl. I could be rolling around in the dirt in jeans at 4:00, and give a piano recital at 7:00 dressed in a pretty pink dress.

13

It never occurred to me that there was a contradiction between being strong and being feminine. I thought I could be anything and everything I wanted.

My high school, which was nationally renowned for its academic and athletic excellence, was very competitive. You were expected to be well dressed, physically fit, and get straight A's. A beauty queen with poor grades was considered a loser. The benefit of having so much demanded of us was that we were instilled with the confidence that we could meet any challenge.

I guess what made me different from my friends, most of whom came from wealthy families with fewer children, were the values I got from my parents. My mom and dad took me out of the comfortable suburbs, into the inner city, to bring food to the urban needy through church-sponsored programs. They made sure we got involved with inner-city kids so we'd know racial and ethnic diversity. The message to us was always, "Listen, you snot-nosed kids, just because you have half an acre around your house and these kids don't even have half a room to call their own, doesn't mean you're any better. What it means, in fact, is that there's so much more you have to do for your community."

After high school, I attended Lake Forest College in Illinois. My major was economics, with a minor in French literature. I hated sitting in a classroom, and thought that it was ridiculous to get A's just because I knew how to regurgitate facts that I memorized. College seemed so remote from real life.

To get the academic credit I needed and the hands-on experience I craved, I devised an independent study project that allowed me to work in a legal aid clinic. There, I saw what real people had to deal with on a day-to-day basis: being locked out of their apartments by landlords who wanted to raise rents, not getting unemployment or workmen's compensation when it was deserved and in general being pushed around by an insensitive system. I thought being a lawyer would be a way to change things, but I soon learned that most attorneys are nothing but glorified paper shufflers.

With my career plans in the air, I decided to fulfill my childhood dream of moving to New York City. I had fond memories of my family's yearly visits to the Big Apple. Since both my parents had grown up there, they were familiar with the city's best and treated us to it. There were shopping trips to Saks Fifth Avenue, Bonwit Teller and Bergdorf Goodman, and lunches at Rumpelmayer's on Central Park South. I thought New York was the most fabulous place in the world.

My main concern about moving to the city was not crime, but keeping my options open. I did not want to be tied down to a job I hated just so I could pay some outrageous rent. I did temporary office work and found the roach-and-rat-infested tenement apartment on Manhattan's Lower East Side where I still live. What the apartment lacked in amenities was more than made up for in the vitality and diversity of the neighborhood.

Friends and relatives warned me to avoid the subway and stay off the streets at night. They forecast that I'd be mugged and raped, and my apartment would be burglarized before I even got the phone installed. I rejected their well-intentioned "advice" and, out of sheer stubbornness, refused to let myself be intimidated by their paranoia. Still, I had to face the fact that I had no idea what to do if I was attacked or robbed.

My bravado faded very fast in the grim reality that faced me every morning just past my door: junkies nodding out in my hallway, drug dealers conducting a brisk out-of-state business on the curb, "stick-up kids" trying to quickly sell gold chains to working people like myself and punks on every corner. I had to learn how to deal with the slime before it consumed me.

After asking just about everyone I knew, finally an acquaintance recommended an excellent martial arts instructor, Sensei Chaka Zulu. His teaching emphasized a Japanese-American hard and soft karate combined with the best techniques from other styles and disciplines. Unlike many martial arts teachers, who concentrate mainly on art form perfection or winning trophies, Sensei Zulu's bottom line was always, Will it work on the streets?

I'll never forget the first time I was knocked down in class. A guy punched me so hard in the solar plexus I was practically knocked out. I had never been hit so hard, and started to cry. Sensei Zulu came over and said, "You can cry all you want, but just don't lay there and take that." So, even though I knew nothing about martial arts, I began fighting back. I grabbed my opponent's feet, I scratched him, I bit him. The teacher yelled, "Good! Good! Keep it up!" 15

Eventually they had to pull me off the guy. I had gone totally crazy. But I learned never to give up, even when you're down. That lesson would later prove to be very important to me.

My confidence in the street began to increase. My stride changed, and the punks appeared to approach me with a little more trepidation. Sometimes I ignored them, sometimes I returned their remarks with a smart comment of my own. Within six months, I felt I could handle a physical confrontation.

After a year, though, I got to the point where my martial arts classes seemed very narcissistic. Here were all these guys, flexing their muscles in the mirror and bragging about how they could take on these imaginary opponents, while—right outside the door—crime was just as bad as ever. I thought we should have been using our skills to protect people in the neighborhood, especially the elderly who couldn't take care of themselves. One day I expressed this feeling to one of the guys in class. He asked, "Have you ever heard of the Guardian Angels?"

2

GUARDIAN ANGEL

Although the name "Guardian Angels" immediately appealed to me, I was not really sure what the group did. My friend explained, "They're a bunch of people who ride the subways and walk the streets. They make sure things are safe for decent people. They're not associated with the police or anything. They're just regular people who care."

I was very interested. I asked how I could join. He told me to go to some address on University Avenue in the Bronx—that's where the group was headquartered the first year of its existence—and ask for the founder, a guy named Curtis.

So, one night, I put on jeans, boots and a leather jacket—an outfit you can wear anywhere in the city—and got on the number 4 subway train to the Bronx. The number 4 is a horrible subway line. It's filthy and graffiti-covered, and the train shakes like it's coming apart at the hinges. I had never gone that far uptown before, and as the train went farther and farther into the Bronx, I became more and more intimidated. There were guys who looked like they were carrying guns in their pockets. Groups of kids with ghetto-blaster radios smoked reefers. Working people huddled in their seats, looking terrified. The farther uptown we got, the worse it got. By the time I exited at Fordham Road, I was convinced I'd have to use my karate skills just to get out of the subway station.

During the day, Fordham Road is a busy commercial strip. But at night, everything is closed except for the bars and fast-food restaurants. People hang out on the street, drinking beer and wine, and hawking drugs. I could feel their eyes on me as I walked to Guardian Angels headquarters.

The University Avenue apartment was like something out of Beirut: noise, graffiti, holes in the walls. The front door and all the windows were open. People were coming and going like the rush hour crowds at Grand Central Station.

Everyone looked at me when I walked in. "I'm here to join," I said, and they all laughed. "Oh, yeah, you're here to join. Who sent you up here? What kind of joke is this?" I sat down on an old bench, hoping my jeans would protect me from whatever was festering on it, and waited for Curtis. I heard him giving directions in the back room. It was strange that all these tough-looking guys, who seemed like they wouldn't listen to anyone, were hanging on his every word. Then he came out, looked me over and practically spat, "So you want to be a Guardian Angel?" He was unspeakably rude. I thought he was a jerk.

"What are you, a cop?" he asked. "A reporter? We'll find out soon enough. Whatever you are, you probably won't last more than a day or two." I came back with: "If this is how you treat people who come in here to join, I'm surprised you have anybody . . ."

Curtis wasn't fazed. "If you're really serious about joining, come back here tomorrow night at eight," he said. Then, he turned and went on to other business.

The next night, a Friday, I pulled up my hair, took off my makeup and put on heavy basketball sneakers, loose karate pants and a big black sweat shirt. I wore a couple of T-shirts underneath to pad myself from injury. I wanted to look like I meant business. I got back on the number 4 train, ready for any test.

I knew that the Guardian Angels had had a lot of martial arts training, but I wasn't sure to what degree my training was comparable. There was no doubt that they had one advantage over me: they had grown up on the streets and I had not. They seemed like they could deal with anything with complete and total confidence.

My test took place in a small park on University Avenue and Fordham Road. Walking there from headquarters, the Angels all seemed like Bruce Lee's younger brothers. I was really nervous.

Once we were deep in the park, they put me through what we call "the circle of death" test. They all surrounded me. One guy at a time would step out of the circle and attack. I thought, "Too bad I don't have a funeral parlor picked out." There was no way I was going to be able to survive if I stood there and took their punches; some of these guys were really built. So I did the only thing I knew I could do: I threw them. As soon as someone would come at me, I'd grab his arm and flip him, or take his head and hurl him, or sweep my leg under him and knock him across the ground. I wasn't thinking about technique, I was thinking about not being pulverized.

20   I went through the whole circle of guys before they admitted I knew

my stuff. We headed back to headquarters in a somewhat euphoric mood. Everyone wanted me in his patrol; they felt I could handle any situation. I wasn't the first female to ever join the Guardian Angels, but the other girls were kind of macho and I was certainly the most feminine-looking applicant these guys had ever seen.

Of course, Curtis was not as enthusiastic about my abilities as the guys. He said, "Well, you fellas think you want this headache. Go ahead, you can have her." But I was in.

After I went through Guardian Angels training, I began patrolling the subways after work and on weekends. A typical subway patrol has ten to twelve members. We usually have one person in each subway car, and we maintain visual contact through the door panels. The last car on the train often has two Angels. That's the party car, the smoker. You could probably get a contact high from just breathing in the marijuana fumes there. You step into that car and discover it's reunion time for all the creeps. Radios are blasting, the beer and wine are flowing and the Transit Police are nowhere to be found. (They don't sell doughnuts on the subway.) Each stop brings on more troublemakers. Fights break out because some jerk doesn't like the way another dude looked at his girl, or because someone took too big a drag from someone's joint, or too big a sip of someone's wine. That was the car I wanted.

I knew that I could never know as much about Harlem or the South Bronx or Brooklyn as the other Angels, and I admitted it. I told them, "You guys are going to have to teach me absolutely everything." And they gave me a crash course on the streets. I learned everything from street language to urban body language. Most important, I learned the signals, code words and behavior patterns of criminals, which enabled me to plot an effective self-defense strategy.

Within months after joining the Angels, I was assuming more and more responsibilities—taking part in special patrols, speaking engagements. Then in the spring of 1981, when Atlanta was being terrorized by the child murders, Curtis decided to send the Angels down there to start chapters and show people how to defend themselves. I was as surprised as everyone else in the group when he put me in charge.

I took a leave of absence from the art gallery where I was working. We boarded the train to Atlanta, then spent one month working twenty-four hours a day. We patrolled, we taught over one thousand kids how to defend themselves, we met with community groups and we learned how to deal with the press. Over 160 foreign correspondents and out-of-state reporters followed our every move—and told the world about the Guardian Angels.

Back in New York, requests to start chapters flooded our office from all over the country. I went back to work at the art gallery, but after two weeks I said, "Lisa, who are you kidding?" The Guardian Angels offered me the total challenge I wanted. And here was an opportunity for me to really give something to society. Of course, I realized that I wouldn't have a regular salary—since the Angels exist solely on the contributions of others—if I dedicated myself to the organization full time. I didn't care. I quit my job at the gallery with no regrets.

Membership in the group climbed. Today, we have approximately five thousand members in the United States, Canada and Mexico. I originally wanted to make Guardian Angels headquarters into a real office, with filing cabinets and desks. Curtis liked things the way they were—anarchistic, with boxes and papers strewn about. He'd yell at me, "You want the Guardian Angels to be run like the Ford Foundation. Well, I see the Ford Foundation has that beautiful glass-front building, but can you tell me one thing they do? I never saw the Ford Foundation on the subway, or in the South Bronx or in Harlem." I could see Curtis's logic. Although we eventually got a slightly more organized office in Harlem, in the annex building of the *Amsterdam News*—New York's largest black weekly newspaper—I came to understand that the Guardian Angels needed to be run uniquely.

Curtis seemed to me like a machine that gave orders and bailed out the Angels when they had trouble with the authorities. When I sized up people for possible relationships, he didn't even rate. Usually, a woman can tell when a man likes her. With Curtis, I couldn't tell anything.

Yet, as my responsibilities in the organization increased, I started to figure out why he acted the way he did. His priorities were in order: get the job at hand done first—and don't waste time. He was cut-and-dried. He accepted no excuses. When one job was finished, he kept driving on to tackle new challenges. I found myself using his leadership techniques more and more.

I was in California, starting new chapters and teaching women self-defense techniques, when I received a message that Curtis had been badly beaten up in Washington, D.C. His instructions to me were, "Stay in California and finish business." A few days later, he called me at 5 A.M. California time, from his mom's house, where he was recuperating. At first, our conversation was strictly professional, then he went very out of character by getting chatty. I said, "Curtis, I'm exhausted; we're working so hard out here. If you have nothing else to say, I'm going to go now."

"I have one more question," he said.

"What's that?"

"Will you marry me?"

I thought he was joking, so I joked back: "Sorry, I don't plan to marry anyone Polish. I have a nice WASP last name and I want to keep it."

He gave me a typical fat-headed response: "Don't worry. You'll agree."

"This isn't Saudi Arabia," I pointed out. "You can't drag me to the altar."

"I'm gonna marry you," he promised, then hung up.

When the San Francisco chapter reached graduation, Curtis showed up for the ceremony on crutches, in a neck brace. Great, I thought, he's here to rain on my parade. It was obvious that he was very ill. His skin was a sickly green color, and he smelled like he had been molding in a closet. "The reason I came here is because I want you to be my wife," he told me.

I told him to go back to New York.

A few days later, he collapsed from exhaustion at a Sacramento radio station. I was afraid that one of the Angels' enemies might try to get to him while he was unconscious, so I ran to his hospital room to post a twenty-four-hour guard. Every few hours, he'd wake up, ask me if I changed my mind, then go back to sleep. And as he slept, I began to consider his question. True, Curtis wasn't the type of guy every little girl in the suburbs dreamed of marrying, but I realized I wasn't the typical suburban girl. I did respect Curtis tremendously. 23

Despite our arguments, I found myself admiring him. And, over the months, I had come to love him too. When he recovered, I accepted his proposal.

The wedding took place on Christmas Eve, 1981. We chose the Judson Memorial Church, across from Washington Square Park in Greenwich Village, for the ceremony. At the time, we had a headquarters in the basement there. Both of our families said they'd boycott the wedding if we wore the T-shirt and red beret that is the Guardian Angels uniform. My father said, "I will give you away, but I want my daughter in a dress and heels. Look like a lady." I agreed. Four hundred Angels showed up in their uniforms, though. When we kissed, they exuberantly tossed their berets up in the air. The local news programs had a field day with that scene.

The next day, we were meeting at the Judson headquarters with some of our people to coordinate patrols and distribution of food to the homeless on New York City's streets. Our Newark, New Jersey, leader, Frank Melvin, a twenty-six-year-old father of three, stopped by with a wedding gift: a pair of jackets like the ones his group wore when they patrolled the Dayton Housing Projects. Less than a week later, as Curtis and I were returning from our "honeymoon" in the drug war–torn Vaughan Housing Projects of St. Louis, we received an urgent call. Frank Melvin was shot dead, for no apparent reason, by a Newark police officer.

When we got married, Curtis and I had committed ourselves not only to each other but to our work. At a time when most newlyweds are still opening their wedding gifts and getting their photo albums back from the studio, we were thrust into the middle of a crisis that separated us. While Curtis was leading a march from Newark to Washington, D.C.—during the coldest winter in seventy-five years—to demand an investigation into Frankie's slaying, I stayed in New York and ran the organization. In the months that followed, our personal life was put on hold. As Curtis and I started chapter after chapter around the country we were rarely in the same city. We lived hand to mouth, subsisting on wedding gifts, Curtis's savings from his former job as a restaurant manager and loans from relatives; all Guardian Angels contributions went to the organization. To this day, neither of us draws a salary. Monumental phone bills and traveling expenses strapped us badly for money. In 1984, when French *Vogue* asked me to model for a special issue on New York City, I said, "Here's a possible solution for our financial dilemma."

We've also been able to supplement our income by lecturing at colleges and universities. As I continue to work with the Guardian Angels—which remains the number-one priority in my life—I hope to develop a career as a professional wrestler.

I've had the opportunity to meet women from every level of American society. As crime increases in areas once considered immune to the epidemic, we have been called upon to share our expertise at handling violent situations. To fill this need, we created the Guardian Angels Street Survival Seminars, which we have offered to urban, suburban and rural women in community centers, church basements, school gymnasiums, shopping malls and city plazas from coast to coast. Through these exchanges and experiences accumulated from thousands of hours of patrolling our nation's most violent places, I have come to know which self-defense techniques work and which don't.

I feel women today ought to consider themselves an endangered species. To prevent extinction, it is necessary to understand the laws of the predators and separate sound practices from bogus advice of "experts"—many of them men who pack at least one .45-caliber "equalizer." The truth is that there is no one "right" way to handle threatening situations. This book offers you a wardrobe of options from which you can choose the techniques that best fit you.

3

MENTAL MUSCLE

If you want to understand a woman's confusing predicament, look at twelve- and thirteen-year-old girls. Most already have fully developed figures, know how to dress, do their hair and put on makeup. They know how to make themselves into perfect sexual packages, but do not know how to handle advances from men. This is because they don't know *who* they are. Their role models are the nerf-brained, pearly toothed, peroxide-haired babies depicted in the media, some of whom are known to us simply because they sleep with a famous performer. And we wonder why teenage pregnancies are epidemic!

Every American grows up seeing women objectified. Products from carburetors to yogurt to cigarettes are sold using sex or some distorted concept of female beauty. The same is true for movies, from "high" art to sleazy porn. Women are usually portrayed as the victims, the grand prizes or mindless decorations who supposedly mean yes when they say no.

questionable role models

The names of our beauty queens change, but their stories are similar. One year, a new starlet is on top of the world. The next year, we discover that she has a drug and/or alcohol problem. She checks herself into a celebrity clinic to dry out. Then, she's back in the spotlight, telling the world about how she overcame her addictions. The message is that you can take drugs and get away with it without having to pay a price.

The beauty queens who don't fit this mold still offer no guidance to women living in the real world. Diana, the princess of Wales, is an example. She is an anachronism, a frivolous fantasy who seems content to fulfill the expectation that she look pretty and keep her mouth shut. In reality, she seems like an aristocratic sponge who supports her life of luxury with taxpayers' hard-earned money.

Another media-magnified celebrity who sends mixed signals to teenage girls is Brooke Shields. She is held up as a model of a devoted daughter and claims at age twenty to be a virgin. Yet her devoted mother had her pose for erotic nude photographs at age ten, and in her early teens she played the child prostitute star role in the film *Pretty Baby*.

The television role models are just as poor. Women are usually seen as victims or pathetic incompetents in family dramas. One who isn't—the constantly scheming Alexis, played by Joan Collins, on "Dynasty"—triumphs not because of her talents or inner strength, but because she takes advantage of other people. Her moral is: "Screw others before they have a chance to screw you." As appealing as that may sound, how many women could act that way and still live with themselves?

At the other extreme are the women's movement activists, whose power base is often exaggerated by a controversy-hungry press. I don't think the Equal Rights Amendment failed because of its content. It was defeated because most women were turned off by the angry feminists shouting for its passage.

The women who do deserve to be role models are the ones who juggle work and family responsibilities and still manage to run community and church organizations, who no matter what hardships they face refuse to feel sorry for themselves. Yet they are largely ignored by a media that usually want to celebrate only celebrity.

the guilt dilemma

The women's movement exists mostly in the minds of some East Coast ivory-tower intellectuals whose main function is to give one another awards every year at lavish banquets. They are out of touch with the most urgent problem confronting girls and women today: how to deal with the increasing violence committed against them.

Whether it is unseemly sexual innuendos on the job, catcalls on the street, purse snatchings, assaults or worse, there is no woman who is exempt from the threat of these violations. FBI crime statistics can measure the number of incidents reported but there is no index that can tabulate the emotional price we pay for our fear and frustration.

This is exacerbated by the dilemma of trying to live up to images that either do not exist or are repugnant. Women strive to look great, then they're afraid of the attention their improved appearance attracts; maybe it will incite a rape attempt. It is unfortunate that women frequently feel guilty about the way their good looks "affect" men.

When a man sexually violates a woman—this includes the whole spectrum from the guy at the office who has his arm around her waist and inches it up higher and higher to the guy at a party who won't take no for an answer to the guy who follows her down an alley with the intention of raping her—her typical response is: "Maybe I shouldn't have looked so good. Maybe I shouldn't have worn high heels; I would have been better off with camouflage fatigues and army boots. Maybe, even though it's one hundred and three degrees out, I shouldn't have worn a sleeveless shirt." The guilt makes the victimized woman an accomplice of the people who claim that females "ask" to be abused.

A classic example of this type of scapegoating is the New Bedford, Massachusetts, rape controversy. A woman was raped by at least five men on the pool table of Big Dan's tavern. Local residents told reporters that since the victim walked into a bar at a late hour, she was declaring, "Come take advantage of me!" There was no justification for the rapists' behavior, yet few people wanted to blame them. How natural it was to blame the woman!

Some women even feel guilty when men try to make innocent advances. In terms of a cumulative effect, this can be devastating. A friendly action or sincere question from a male stranger about directions or time causes these women to jump.

don't feel guilty

It is important not to be part of the whole stupid cycle of beliefs reinforcing the victimization of women. We should not feel guilty! If we want to look good, that's our choice. To feel responsible for someone who wants to take advantage of us is ridiculous. That only gives credibility to the creep.

Sexual crimes do not occur because men "get an itch." If that was the case, eighty-seven-year-old women wouldn't be raped by sixteen-year-old boys. Sexual criminals are not following their libidos, but lusting for power. From the casual molester at the office water cooler to the rapist, these men are insecure about their masculinity and ability to get women to pay attention to them—much less go to bed with them. So they've developed a hatred for women that manifests itself in various ways. Making an unwanted sexual advance is one way of getting even with women. If the creep succeeds in intimidating a woman, that gives him a thrilling sense of power.

be prepared

Understanding the sexual criminal will not make the problem disappear. Sexual harassment is unfortunately a part of life. Women must be ready to face a variety of situations.

Preparation for an encounter with a pervert is a necessity. It is like wearing a seat belt. When you strap yourself in, you are not saying, "Today I expect to have a car accident." You just want to be ready, *in case* something occurs. You must develop the same heightened awareness and casualness about self-defense.

Boldness is better than guilt. Say: "Yes, I have what a man wants. But the only way he is going to get it is if I want to give it to him. If someone tries to take something from me against my will, I'm going to take measures to stop him."

recognize your strength

And you can stop him! You must stop believing that women are powerless. Women are told that they are weak and irrational in tense situations. I'm sure everyone has heard the joke about the female president who pushes the button because she's cranky at that time of the month. My response to this type of thinking is that women can never be as irrational as the Pentagon generals who sent our brothers, sons and husbands to Beirut only to lament after many were killed

32

that they weren't quite sure why we were there in the first place.

Though we are led to believe otherwise, women are strong. Females are the bulk and backbone of most community groups and most families. When a crisis arises on the domestic front—a death in the family, a fizzling marriage, a sick child—women often take command, without panicking or breaking down.

If a woman can do things for other people, she can do things for herself. In war, it is not always the biggest army that wins, but the one that has its act together and is thus able to respond immediately and effectively to a crisis.

recognize your fears

Along with recognizing your strength, you must recognize your fears. This means asking "What am I afraid of?" and giving yourself an honest answer. If you feel uncomfortable about riding buses, question, "Why is it that I feel uncomfortable? Do I have a general uneasiness about riding mass transit? Do I have a particular fear when I see a certain type of person on the bus? Am I afraid of having my property stolen? Do I have a fear of being raped? Or am I most afraid of my inability to deal with the unknown?" Many people experience the last fear.

value yourself, not the criminal

If you look at things from a balanced perspective, you will have the attitude to help you triumph. The truth is that you and your possessions are valuable. You work hard for everything you have, and no one has earned the privilege to take it from you. If an acquaintance entered your home and demanded ten dollars, you'd show that person the door. Why should a criminal be afforded any more courtesy?

Do not romanticize the criminal. Most people are intimidated by lawbreakers because they act bold. Criminals are not bold! They are parasites with a distorted view of reality. It is your responsibility to set them straight by saying, "Hey, Jack, your number's up. I know what you're thinking, but you'll never get away with it."

33

remember the good

There are a number of exercises you can do to strengthen your mental posture. One of the best involves focusing on your positive qualities. Whenever you have a moment to yourself, think of something you did within the last twenty-four hours that makes you proud: being especially nice to someone who is lonely, buying a sandwich for a homeless person, standing up for yourself in a personal or work situation, experiencing success at work or school, or helping to make a relationship more satisfying. No matter how trivial your action may seem, if it makes you proud it's important.

If you go through this exercise daily, in time you won't have to force yourself to focus on what's positive about your life. The memories will come naturally and you'll feel like the sum total of all the wonderful things you did (and do) for yourself and others.

A similar exercise, but one that you don't have to do every day, is comparing your situation now to what it was a year or two ago. Think about those things you believed you couldn't do, the things today you know you've conquered: losing unwanted pounds, quitting smoking, cutting back on drinking or drugs, getting your own apartment, moving to a different city, surviving a bad relationship. Once you had made up your mind, you *were* able to do what you intended. These were times when you took charge, when you weren't afraid to direct yourself, when your methods worked. Just as you've overcome seemingly impossible obstacles in the past, you can continue to change your life for the better now and in the future.

derail delayed reactions

The best way to deal with a problem is straight on, but not head on so as to cause a collision. Yet many women find themselves falling victim to delayed-reaction anger and get upset about an event a few days or weeks afterward. Being in touch with your immediate feelings, especially anger, is essential to successfully handling crises, particularly violent ones.

Here's a typical delayed-reaction scenario: You come into the office with a cake you baked or bought for a party. There are six pieces, one for each person in the company. The office pig comes over and grabs two servings for himself. You notice this, but don't want to make waves, so you don't eat one. You feel like you cheated yourself, however, because you let this inconsiderate pig have his way without calling him on it. The resentment you feel toward him builds as you recall how you went without breakfast so you could splurge on the cake. The next time you deal with him, the delayed-reaction anger erupts over something inconsequential, which makes you look irrational and irresponsible—the living stereotype of the woman who goes crazy and out of control every time the heat is on.

Don't wait for the anger to build up. Put him in his place *when* he deserves it. Don't grab the cake from him, just coolly throw out a line like, "What are you trying to be, the Pillsbury dough boy?"

When this type of situation is dealt with on the spot, it does not seem as monumental as it does in retrospect. And your words don't take on an emotional charge that makes you appear unbalanced.

Although you may think the other person will end up hating you, he'll probably respect you for catching him. Anyone who is doing something wrong, whether it's an office pig or a criminal, is ultraconscious of the fact that he or she is trying to sneak by. Being caught in the act puts a total chink in their plan of action.

Even a simple deed, like standing up to a pest at work, helps you see that you can handle whatever arises, and also helps to develop the instantaneous reactions and confidence you may need one day to survive a life-threatening situation. With the road before you largely uncharted territory and with few practical role models as guides, you must focus on your powers and innate skills in order to build strength within yourself—and set examples for other women.

4

INSIDE A SUBSPECIES: THE CRIMINAL MIND

In this society, the little girl who sells the most cookies for charity does not make headlines, but the woman who kills her lover does. The male cult hero is not the boy who pulls a family from a burning building, but the maniac who takes eight hostages in a bank. The media provide a sounding board for these "luminaries" after apprehension; the suspects often request which news correspondents they want to speak with. If the crime committed is particularly heinous, the perpetrator is glorified by famous authors who apparently view the destruction of life as some manifestation of masculinity.

Thus, many youngsters grow up dreaming of turning their dark fantasies into grizzly realities. With little guidance other than the television set—which has projected sixteen thousand murders to the average person by the time he or she is eighteen years old—few alternatives to the criminal path are offered. A large percentage of lawbreakers come from broken homes; some spent most of their young lives being shuttled from one household to another. In addition to suffering abuse as children, they witnessed adults abusing themselves and each other. These children were never given standards of behavior or self-worth. By their early teens, they have a value system that condones theft, harassment and assault, in which the prevailing mentality is, Get what you want right away, no matter what the consequences. They see their own lives as having little value, and have even less respect for yours.

the criminal "look"

Many goons dress the way they do to inspire fear in normal, hard-working citizens. Their choice of clothing is an act of defiance against conventional society. The posture is no different from that of pirates, who advertised their status as outcasts by sporting bandanas, eye patches, wild boots, vests and earrings.

An inner-city punk will wear a pop-up hat, expensive sneakers with color-coordinated laces, pounds of gold chains—which you know he didn't buy on the installment plan—and, during the winter, a large sheepskin coat, into which he sticks his hand to appear like he's packing a piece. Large glasses give him an "other world" look, as if he just transferred onto your subway train from a spaceship.

In the suburbs, variations of the *Road Warrior* look are found: black leather, large boots, torn-up jeans, earrings, dangling chains. Heavy-metal fans are partial to long hair, bandanas and patches naming their favorite bands.

Sometimes a car is part of the look. Suburban kids hanging out in a customized auto, with the music blasting, are telling passersby: This is a rowdy crowd.

Rural hoodlums are fond of hiking boots, down vests, long hair, beards and, above everything, bright hunter's colors. There is no mistaking their message, It's open season on chumps.

The deviant look is sometimes complemented by a can of beer. When a thug has the beverage in his hands, he is lounging; he intends to remain where he stands for a while. Like a buzzard or a vulture, he is waiting for a good morsel to pick.

"group" psychology

Punks everywhere are the same in that they feel most confident surrounded by their cronies in a familiar setting, usually the parking lot of a fast-food restaurant or mall, public park or street corner. An essential prop for their act is the boom-box radio. In case you are able to ignore the group members' flamboyant dress and rowdy behavior, the loud beat causes you to pay attention to and possibly fear them. Occasionally, they are accompanied by a few groupie girls.

The more members of a group, the more cowardly each individual generally is. This does not mean that you should dismiss the threat they pose. Chickenhearted or not, these people can be dangerous if they decide to vent their frustrations and anger on you.

handling groups

When you encounter a creepy group of guys, do not question, "Am I prejudging these people because of how they look?" Follow your instincts. That's what animals do to alert themselves to danger, and that's why they survive.

Do not ignore the classic criminal stereotypes: ninety percent of the people in prison probably fit them. Ignoring appearance because you want to be fair is being unfair to yourself.

Acknowledging potential danger does not always mean getting physical. It is like manning a radar screen. When you notice an object on the screen, you rarely fire the missiles. You simply take notice, track the object and ready yourself to combat it.

It's better to be cautious and then safely assured that you made a mistake than to be attacked when your guard is down.

cross the street

A woman who has misgivings about a group she sees ahead of her is often hesitant to avoid them by crossing the street. She thinks the action will reveal her fear. So she continues walking—right into the heart of the jungle. And, like jungle animals, the thugs smell her fear and pounce. Their attitude is, If you're stupid enough to walk by us, you deserve to be mugged.

If you find yourself in this situation, do not hesitate to cross the street. The hoodlums will see that you have no desire to play their game. Your action will be taken not as a sign of fear, but rejection, conveying your attitude that no one has the right to bother you.

passing the group

If, for some reason, you walk past a rowdy group, they may try a number of gimmicks to test your fear factor. These jerks have 41 probably been standing in the same place all day. The longer they stand, the more antsy they get. An out-of-the-ordinary reaction from a passerby provides them with a situation comedy to step into.

The leader of the group may step out and ask you questions. As naturally as possible, reply that you're in a hurry and do not have the time to talk. *Do not allow yourself to be stopped!*

Another intimidation tactic is loud language, sometimes with sexual innuendo. They're looking for an extreme reaction. If you flinch, you will be pegged as easy bait. If you berate them, they have a new character to play with. Choosing to joust verbally is encouraging trouble. The punks have done this hundreds of times and have control of the lines. They're already wound up like tops; if you pull the string, you don't know where they'll spin.

It is best to act indifferent and keep walking.

Silent methods of intimidation include bold walking, roughhousing and staring. Bold walking—usually stomping and swaggering—is done to back up the hoodlums' antisociety image. The message of the roughhousing—pushing, punching and shoulder-blocking—is: We're doing this to each other now, but we could be doing it to you soon. The purpose of the stare is to measure your fear and unnerve you to the point where you let down your guard. The thugs are also observing you to determine how familiar you are with your surroundings. It is impossible to engage in stares with everyone you meet, yet you can't ignore glaring rays as if you were a horse with blinders. You do not want to appear overly aggressive or passive. Respond to stares—as well as other methods of silent intimidation— with apparent boredom. Act as if you've seen these routines before, and now you're just browsing. You may be terrified, but you must become a good character actor in order to avert crime. Otherwise, you run the risk of becoming the first act of a one-act tragedy.

being followed

If you are followed by any of these goons, do not lead them to your car or home. Keep calm and look for a place where there are other people: a newsstand, gas station or store. If the thugs wait for you outside, call the police.

criminals who don't look the part

Of course, not all criminals fit into the categories described (likewise, not every inner-city youth in a sheepskin coat or suburban kid who looks like an extra in an AC/DC video is a lawbreaker). The professional criminal may go out of his or her way to blend into the working territory. In a business district, pickpockets and rapists may wear three-piece suits. In the shopping mall, some thieves look like typical working men or women. By fearing one type of person, but not another, you are more likely to fall victim to crime. No group understands this better than police officers. When you are stopped for even a minor traffic violation, cops approach your car from both sides, shining flashlights and sometimes fingering triggers. This is done no doubt because too many trusting officers have been blown away by nuts who looked "normal."

young criminals

Sadly, children cannot be dismissed as innocents either. The average age of those committing petty crimes continues to get lower in urban areas, particularly in New York City. If you are on the subway and see children running up and down the aisles, their frolicking may not be as innocent as you'd like to believe. It is likely that their goal is snatching pocketbooks, wallets and jewelry. Young hoodlums are crafty enough to realize that their age offers many onlookers a false sense of security.

alcohol- and drug-induced crime

When people are drunk or stoned, they may revert back to their animal nature—it doesn't matter if they are cops, physicians or politicians. How many times have we seen our own relative turn from Mary Poppins to Attila the Hun because of a drink, joint or pill? The list of people raped and assaulted by friends and relatives under the influence is endless.

Similarly, winos and inebriated transients shouldn't be disregarded. Not all homeless people are the sedate folks about whom TV movies are made. Many should be in mental institutions. The consumption of alcohol or drugs does not always have a calming effect on them.

When you see someone who is drunk or stoned, do not panic, but be wary. It is no different from driving late at night and observing the car in front of you weaving. You avoid passing the vehicle if you can out of precaution rather than terror. If the other driver could see your face in his rearview mirror, he'd observe not a paranoid maniac, but a careful motorist cruising along.

keep sharp

In day-to-day life, it is futile to play analyst, putting criminals on the couch. But if you know your enemy, it will be easier to put him on the asphalt if the circumstances deem necessary.

5

EVERY WOMAN'S DECISION

Women expend tremendous energy taking care of the way they look—the latest hairstyles, makeup and the newest diets are crucial issues. As a model, I'm as guilty as everyone else. If so much emphasis is placed on appearance, it is ridiculous not to give some thought to crime, which is the greatest threat to our physical safety and well-being.

Before you start thinking about self-defense, though, you must take a long, hard look at yourself. Take this test to see if you are a charter member of the Victim's Club:

1. Do you get more angry at yourself than at other people?
2. Do you blame yourself for your failures but fail to take responsibility for changing your circumstances?
3. Do you lose your cool when you don't mean to?
4. When something bad or discouraging happens, do you tell yourself, "That's just my luck"?
5. Do you put yourself down when somebody pays you a sincere compliment?

If you answered yes to any of these questions, you are shortchanging yourself. Your emotional and psychological makeup means you are a likely crime victim. However, like everyone, you have what it takes to change your condition. It's a matter of *making the decision* to think differently; realizing that your life, your body and your property are worth fighting for.

By examining each question, the solutions become evident:

1. *Do you get more angry at yourself than at other people?*

Why do you get angry—because of what happened or because you didn't stand up for yourself when it did? A person who feels she compromised herself by not speaking up is an angry person. Use the delayed-reaction scenario in chapter three as a reference, and start asserting yourself.

2. Do you blame yourself for your failures but fail to take responsibility for changing your circumstances?

Instead of focusing on what you view as your shortcomings, build confidence by concentrating on the things you like about yourself. Take steps—they don't have to be giant ones—to change the self-deprecating way you deal with people in relationships and in the workplace. For example, if you are involved with a man who expresses indifference toward you, turn the tables on him. The next time he asks you for a date, tell him, "I can't go out that night. I'm busy." *Even if it hurts!* That's a positive switch from keeping your plans suspended until he decides when he wants to get together. At work, assert yourself when asked to do another job to cover up for an employee who is slacking off. Say: "Look, I'm happy you think I'm capable of doing this task, but it would be impossible with the work load I already have." As long as you are truly being overworked, you have every right to request fair treatment.

3. Do you lose your cool when you don't mean to?

When you do not put your foot down at the right moment, your anger can often end up misdirected. You are angry at your boss, but you explode at your child. When you blow up at the wrong time, or at the wrong person, you feel worse because you reinforce your belief that you cannot control your emotions. The answer is to simply confront problems when they occur. When taken in the right context, they are usually manageable—and you save yourself emotional wear and tear.

4. When something bad or discouraging happens, do you tell yourself, "That's just my luck"?

"Just my luck" is an unrealistic cop-out that serves only to bring you down. What you are saying is, "Nothing good ever happens to me, and when it does, it's a fluke." In the meantime, you ignore positive strokes of luck, like catching a bus two seconds before it leaves the station. If you acknowledge both negative *and* positive strokes of luck, things will seem balanced.

5. Do you put yourself down when somebody pays you a sincere compliment?

Because of the stress this society places on superficial beauty, women are far too critical of themselves, and judge themselves far more harshly than anyone else might. Nowhere is this more apparent than in the modeling business. At job interviews—or "go-sees" as they're called—anywhere from two to twenty models wait in a room to show themselves and their portfolios to prospective employers. Even though they are the cream of the crop of beauty, many will swear that they are ugly and will compare themselves unfavorably with everyone else in the room. By doing this, instead of concentrating on their good points, they make themselves miserable and reinforce their insecurities.

Women love to torture themselves this way. When a man says, "You look beautiful tonight," most think, "How can that be? I just had a piece of cheesecake and I feel like a blimp," or "What is he trying to get from me?" Rarely do they contemplate the possibility that they *do* look beautiful.

Once again, you should be concentrating on what you have instead of what you're lacking. When you look in the mirror, don't say, "There's that ugly nose again." Say: "There are those great eyes and fantastic smile." It sounds simplistic, but your face and body respond to that type of stroking.

make the commitment

No matter how many self-defense "ribbons" you possess—a black belt in karate, a black sash in kung fu, a certificate of completion from a soldier-of-fortune survival school—your physical skills are worthless if you have the wrong attitude. If physical know-how was all that mattered, martial arts trainees wouldn't be mugged as frequently as they are, and eighty-year-old women wouldn't be able to successfully fend off attackers.

Old age is usually associated with vulnerability. However, even very senior citizens have successfully fought off muggers because they were not willing to give up anything to a punk. Their decision to fight back compensated for whatever infirmities they had.

49

If more people had their attitude, the crime rate would drop. If every woman was committed to saying, "Enough is enough!"—with her mouth, fists and nails—thugs would think before they terrorized. Making this type of promise to yourself will increase your confidence about encountering criminals and reduce the likelihood that they'll be attracted to you.

Through talking to thousands of women around the country at self-defense seminars, I've found that, even among those who sustained injuries or loss of property, crime victims who battled their assailants were left with fewer psychological scars than those who did nothing. The women who fought back knew they hadn't submitted totally, thus their self-esteem was not destroyed.

fear

A typical exchange I have at a seminar goes something like this:

"Lisa, the whole idea of a violent confrontation scares me so much. How could I even think of striking an attacker?"

"Well, ask yourself this. When you walk on the street, are you ever afraid?"

"Yes, I'm afraid *all* the time."

"Do you like that feeling of fear?"

"No, I wish there was something I could do about it."

"There is. Decide that you don't want to live with it anymore, that you want to get to the root cause of the fear and the understanding that what you're really afraid of is not so much the attack but the idea that you don't know how to handle yourself. Therefore, you have no confidence in how you'd handle the situation."

The fears you carry are exacerbated by daily harassments. Because you don't know how to handle harassment, you try to ignore it, hoping desperately no harm will come to you. The constant choice not to take a stand eats away at your self-confidence; the fear spreads faster and is more voracious in its appetite than cancer. The criminals, who check women out to determine their fear levels, find easy marks. When you are grabbed, all your fears and emotions erupt like a volcano. Because you don't know what to expect or do, you are rendered paralyzed.

adaptability

Most street parasites believe it is female nature to yield. This tenet, unfortunately, is based on some degree of truth: women have been trained to adapt. If there's a conflict of power at work or in a relationship, females are expected to play the honey, to sacrifice their own feelings and ambitions.

Female willingness to yield is so extreme that excuses for those who perpetrate violence against women are accepted. I was outraged over a recent theory called "rapism." According to the male psychiatrist who conceived the notion, the desire to rape is a mental illness. This means that the sickos who rape now have a new psychological defense when their cases are tried. It's time for the brainiacs to stop inventing new excuses for criminal behavior!

it's up to you

Female "emotional dinosaurs" should be made as extinct as those stuffed reptiles in the museum. Who is an emotional dinosaur? It's a woman who says, "If I stand up for myself, if I rock the boat, nobody's gonna love me and I'll be left alone." Well, ultimately everyone is alone anyway. Even if you are in a loving relationship, you must face life's challenges by yourself.

No female, whether she's two or eighty-two, is exempt from the violations that have become so commonplace in this society. You can blame men, your mother, rock videos and pornography for the increasing violence women face. And while you're pointing your finger, someone is going to grab your behind and try to knock you on the ground. You are thinking archaically unless you accept that fighting violence against women is *your* responsibility.

If you want the choice of life-style, education and mobility—to have all the opportunities our grandmothers didn't—recognize that there are many negative things in a society so permissive. One of those things is crime. You must deal with it!

give him pain

Pain is sometimes the only thing a criminal understands. You have to be willing to inflict it. I understand that many women are hesitant to do this, but what other choices are there? If a man has his hands on your throat, forget about reasoning with him. Many minor crimes against women end up being combination crimes; a thug meets no resistance when he demands a purse, so he rapes. Using force to extinguish the criminal's power is the only alternative you have.

Because most men are stronger than most women, I don't propose tests of strength or hour-long slugfests. Hit and run. After striking an attacker, do not wait around to see his reaction. Just put him in pain, and get away.

know you'll fight

You should convince yourself *before* a crime situation occurs that you'll fight the criminal, and be committed to battle *regardless of the consequences*. This is the only attitude that's going to make you win. If you wait to decide whether to fight *when* the criminal accosts you, you're greatly increasing your chances of defeat.

Don't expect each blow to hit its desired target; not every technique you use will work. But once you start fighting, you can't stop; you have to go all the way. And—this phrase never applied more appropriately—if at first you don't succeed, try, try again.

get physical

Serious attacks against women do not always begin brutally. Often, they start with a man looking you in the eye, placing his hand on your shoulder and talking. The hand slides down your arm and the assault escalates from there. A common mistake many women make is *asking*, "Could you please stop?" without doing anything physically in return.

This response rarely works because men have been weaned

on the belief that when a woman says no, she really means yes.

A physical action demands a physical response. The way to get your wishes across so they can be understood even by a subgrade moron is to take his hand off your shoulder and say, "Get lost."

The degree of your response should depend on the seriousness of the approach. If you know the man with his hand on your shoulder, simply removing the offensive paw might be enough. If he refuses to relent, a knee in the groin will clarify your desires.

There are no rigid guidelines on how to fend off assaults. Every situation is unique. Here are some of the more common scenarios:

the office molester

The office molester is partial to "mild" assaults. He puts his arm around you in an apparent gesture of company camaraderie, but his fingers can't stay far from your breasts. You can't scream and create a scene in the office the way you would in a public place, and he may be responsible for signing your checks. What you must do is physically take his hand off you, giving him a clear admonishment: "You can look, but you can't touch." You can do it with a smile, even with a joke: "I realize you're the sex symbol of the office, but I'm very much in love with my boyfriend. Maybe the other women will better appreciate your charms." Your message will be conveyed and—since most of these guys are cowards—he'll probably never bother you again.

date rape

There are few crimes people enjoy blaming on victims as much as date rape. The victims themselves often believe they are obligated to have sex with their assailants. A woman will tell herself, "Well, this man put out so much money tonight. I owe him something." The man, in turn, thinks, "I put out. Now she'll put out."

If you allow yourself to get caught up in this manner of thinking, you are nothing more than a prostitute. Your body is yours to give to

53

whomever *you* want whenever *you* want. Choosing to follow this philosophy is an important step in combatting date rape.

You do not owe the man anything sexual for his money. He paid for the privilege of your company! If you're called a bitch for thinking this way, fine. It's better to be a bitch than to submit to somebody else's sexual demands.

By projecting this self-valuing attitude, you send out very decipherable signals to your date to be a gentleman. If he refuses to read those signals, and attempts to physically coerce you into bed with him, treat him no differently than a back-alley rapist (more on how to battle the rapist later).

street harassment

Every woman experiences street harassment; some must endure it seven days a week. Hoots of "Hey, baby, you look so fine!" might make you feel like punching a man's teeth down his throat, but—if he is not making any physical moves toward you—it is more practical for you to act as if you haven't heard him. By acknowledging him, you are giving him what he craves: attention.

groups

Beware of groups of guys who try to stop you with a question: "Do you have a match? Do you have the time?" Do not allow yourself to be stopped. Without breaking stride, reply, "No, I don't have a match. I don't smoke," or "No, I don't have the time. My watch is broken." As long as you keep walking, they will not be able to corner you.

the weapon-wielder

When someone is threatening you with a weapon, your utmost concern should be avoiding injury. Still, you have to be committed to finding a way out of the situation. A rapist holding a knife at your throat must, at some point, put down the blade. That's your cue—your room to move. The next chapter will discuss "techniques of last resort" that can be applied in this situation.

Again, the right attitude here is really the key to your survival. It was Corazon Amurao's attitude—her refusal to yield and be violated—that saved her from certain death. Around midnight on July 13, 1966, she opened her bedroom door in the Chicago townhouse she shared with other nursing students to discover Richard Speck, a pock-marked drifter from Texas, waving a gun at her. The trainee from the Philippines was forced to join eight housemates in one of the bedrooms. Speck assured the women that he only wanted money for a trip to New Orleans and had no intention of harming them. He asked each woman where she kept her money, then bound and gagged them with sliced-up bed sheets.

When Speck briefly left them alone, Amurao pleaded with the others to team up and overtake him. Another Philippina, Merlita Gargullo, agreed, but the rest of the nurses were too frightened. They were willing to submit to rape, hoping that would satisfy the intruder enough not to kill them. Determined not to be defiled, Amurao rolled under a bunk bed, praying that Speck hadn't counted his victims. She listened as he led each girl out of the room. The next morning, after no one turned off a ringing alarm clock, Amurao was confident that Speck had gone. She rolled out from under the bed and discovered her eight friends' stabbed and strangled corpses.

Corazon Amurao understood that a criminal's assurances are bogus. She appreciated her self-worth and was willing to make a decision based on it. That decision saved her life. A similar one could save yours.

6

MOVES MOTHER NEVER TAUGHT YOU

A man's size and strength are understandably frightening to most women. No one is invincible, however, not even a giant. Brute force does not automatically determine the victor in a fight. Remember David and Goliath? By using your instincts and savvy, you can fend off an attacker long enough to give yourself a chance to get away. The strategy is to avoid getting into a brawl where you are at a distinct disadvantage. Instead, you strike the most vulnerable areas of a man's body and inflict enough pain to divert his attention, buying the precious moments you need to get away.

Here are some of the most effective areas to strike:

eyes Use your fully extended fingers, a knuckle or a pointy object—such as a pen—to poke your attacker's eyes, robbing his vision. If he can't see you, he can't hurt you. Remember to hit and run; leave after blinding.

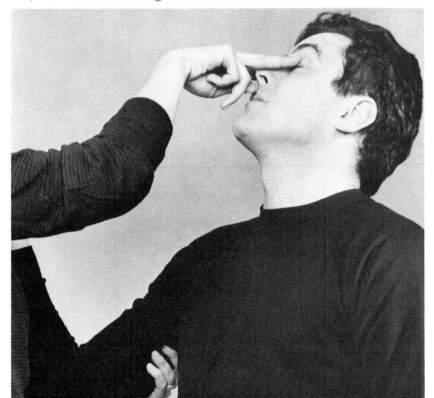

hair Use an assailant's hair to force his head into a hard surface. Grab him by the locks and bang his head against the ground, a tree, a wall, anything that is close and won't give.

ears Press your fingers together tightly, cup both your hands and smack them (one over each ear) over the attacker's ears. The "suction cup" action causes great pain.

behind the earlobes

Place a finger behind each earlobe and press the soft area where the neck muscle meets the jaw bone. By pushing on this pressure point, you can steer your attacker's head wherever you wish—away from you or into a wall.

the tip of the nose

Hit the fleshy tip of the nose with the heel of your palm, pushing upward. The result can be permanent brain damage.

face

Scratch the skin with your nails, pinch it and, if nothing else is possible, bite wherever you can.

throat

Any strike to the Adam's apple—with a closed fist, elbow or hard object—is extremely painful. If enough force is exerted, the tubes beneath the windpipe will break, breathing will be cut off and the attacker will be rendered unconscious.

above the collarbone

At the base of the throat, there is a tissue-thin inverted area. Pushing the spot with a fingertip or knuckle will seriously injure the criminal.

fingers

When seized from behind, do not waste the energy required to muscle out. Instead, peel the punk's fingers back as far as you can, snapping them out of joint. The pain will force him to let go, enabling you to spin around and strike.

groin An excellent place to hit, not first, but second. Most attackers *expect* a kick to the groin and will move to protect the area. Blind your assailant first, then go after his genitals. Using your knee to hit this target is better than kicking. The striking surface of the foot is smaller than that of the knee, you run the risk of breaking your toes and it's more difficult to keep your balance.

knees
If you are carrying a heavy bag, slam it into the thug's knees. A kick is also good (more on how to use your feet later in this chapter).

shins
As you undoubtedly know from nicking them on table edges, the shins are very tender. A kick to the shins hurts and allows you to stay low, maintaining your balance.

instep of the foot
A great area to strike when assaulted from behind. The instep is weak and can be easily broken by a smashing heel. Someone with a broken foot can't chase you.

These are the choice striking spots. Two areas to avoid are the torso and solar plexus. The torso is usually the strongest part of a man's body and difficult to damage. The solar plexus is hard to find and strike effectively. However, you must inflict pain on whichever part of the body is closest to you. Always, the idea is to get away as soon as your attacker's attention is off you.

where to strike from

Every woman's body is stocked with natural weapons. Here is how to use them in your defense:

head
Few criminals expect a woman to administer a head butt. If you have been knocked down and your attacker is standing over you, thrust the crown of your head into the groin. If grabbed from behind, toss your head back into his face, hitting with the top of your skull.

teeth
Bite—anywhere, anything, anytime!

elbows
The "elbow strike" is especially useful when you are attacked from close range. Depending upon your height, the point of your elbow can be thrust upward into the Adam's apple, or jammed down, across your body, into his groin.

fingers
Two fingers, extended apart, can be jabbed into eyes. If your attacker can't see you, he can't get you. Fingernails are good for clawing and pinching.

hips When attacked from the rear, push your hips backward into the criminal's groin area. The move—known as the "hip butt" and "mambo shot"—will throw your assailant off-balance.

hands Pull hair and earlobes. Making a traditional fist is difficult for women who aren't trained fighters. Unless your wrist is straight when you're throwing the punch, you are likely to break it on impact. Use a "hammer fist," hitting with the side of your fist as you swing your arm down. Or raise your fist to your opposite shoulder, swing it outward and hit with the back or side of your hand. Aim for the throat, collarbone or temple.

knees Your knee has a large, hard striking surface. Jam it into a hoodlum's groin. When he doubles over in pain, grab his head—by the hair or the ears—and smash it into your bent knee.

feet Because it's very easy to break your toes, do not kick your attacker with the tip of your foot. Use the "blade edge"—the outer side—to hit the shins and knees. When stomping on an instep—again, do not use your fragile toes. Utilize your powerful heel. If you are wearing high-heeled shoes, that's even better.

in your handbag

I do not recommend packing a gun or knife in your handbag. Aside from the potential for accidents, there is the possibility that you may not find your weapon when a crisis arises. Think of how long it has taken you to fish out a lipstick or comb from your purse. An attacker is not going to wait patiently while you rummage for your dainty .22.

Mace has been lauded as the perfect weapon for women, but I

69

disagree. Aside from being illegal in some states, most of the commercially available Mace-type products are oil-based and do not have the paralyzing effect of the solutions used by police riot squads. The aerosol canisters that house these products frequently malfunction. Putting your life and safety behind these products is not advisable.

A few items commonly found in handbags can be used to stop an attack. Whereas a thug knows the intentions of a woman carrying a knife or gun, and may use the weapon against her, few view keys and compacts as deadly weapons, and you'll have the element of surprise on your side.

keys
Laced between your fingers, keys can achieve the same end as brass knuckles. They can also shred flesh. Attach your keys to an unbreakable plastic or metal rod, which, when placed through your fingers and held tightly, will offer you another striking surface.

hairbrush, pick, unbreakable comb
Use these to scratch facial skin, puncture eyes and rake exposed skin.

breath spray, perfume
You can squirt these in an attacker's eyes. If you've accidentally done this to yourself, you know the sting and how long it takes to see clearly again.

pen
Poke an unbreakable, plastic pen into eyes. Some receptionists have done this when assaulted by madmen trying to enter offices. To imagine the pain caused by a pen, think of all the times you have stabbed yourself with a mascara wand. And that wasn't even done with force!

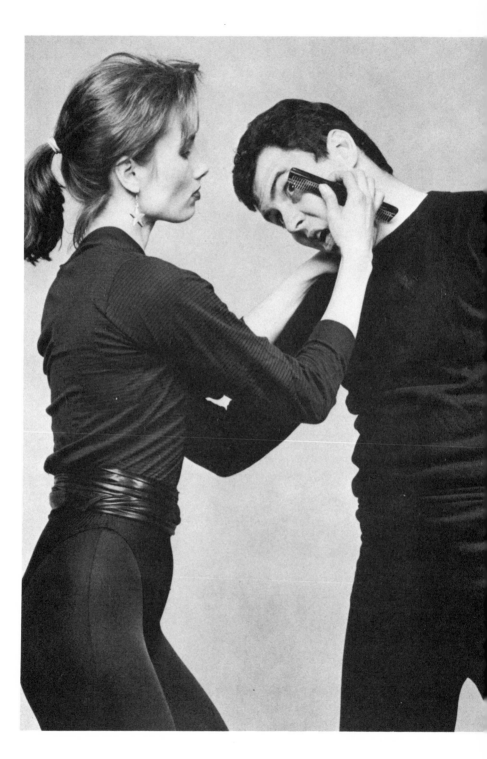

compacts If broken these become jagged glass edges that can be used to cut an attacker.

handbag The handbag itself, often filled with heavy objects, is good for swinging into the side of a criminal's head, knees and groin.

Whatever is in your hands should be used to injure your assaulter.

When purchasing an umbrella, consider its self-defense possibilities. Buy the type of umbrella that collapses down to the length of a nightstick. If necessary, *use* it as a nightstick.

A heavy book shoved into the Adam's apple or groin area is an effective diversion.

combinations

The decision to fight back is one you make yourself. At one extreme are those who tell women to submit passively to every attack. At the opposite extreme are those who would like to see us turned into armed guerrillas. By yielding to a criminal's demands, you are, in effect, placing your trust in him—trusting him to take your property and not do you bodily harm. By depending exclusively upon a gun or other weapon, you focus all your attention on an object that is useless (and could be dangerous to you) unless it's in your hands. You cannot survive by putting all your trust or hope in another person—especially a criminal—or weapon. You must trust yourself to believe that you can find a way out.

It's impossible to predict every move a criminal will make. What follows is a list of some of the common criminal approaches and effective countermoves.

73

rear neck grab

While you are unlocking your car or apartment, a hoodlum sneaks up behind you, places his forearm over your neck and slams you against the door. Do not struggle to remove his arm. Turn your head to the side, to ease the pressure on your throat. If you can, pull his arm slightly down. Stomp on his instep with your heel. Kick his shins with the blade of your foot. Since you are close enough to him to feel his body parts, bring your elbow across your chest and into his Adam's apple. Push him away and run.

purse snatching

A thief grabs your purse as you cling to the strap. Many women make the mistake of getting into a tug-of-war. Instead of pulling away, push toward the punk, kicking him in the shins, kneeing him in the groin and using the purse to smash him in the temple. Grab your purse and leave.

Things to remember: work the parts of the attacker's body closest to each other and to you. You may be successful in striking the instep and then the eyes, but the rhythm is better when you go after the eyes and then the throat; if your first technique doesn't work, try another. Once you begin fighting, never stop; in between set maneuvers, kick, bite, scratch and otherwise improvise; hit and run.

frontal grab

A man approaches you and begins to talk, placing a firm hand on your shoulder. You feel threatened; you want to get rid of that hand *and* him. Poke him in the eyes and knee him in the groin. As he doubles over in pain, push him away and run.

shoulder grab

A man stands in front of you and begins to squeeze your shoulders. He expects you to try to move his hands, which would involve a test of strength you'd probably lose. Surprise him by kicking his shins with the outside edge of your foot. Follow with a strike to the throat with the heel of your palm. Grab and squeeze his Adam's apple with your thumb and fingers. If you don't feel he is sufficiently disabled, knee him in the groin. Push him away and run.

rear lift

You are seized from behind, around the waist, and lifted. Peel your attacker's fingers out of joint while kicking furiously at his shins. He'll have to release you because of the pain in both areas.

techniques of last resort

The techniques discussed thus far in this chapter pertain to battling one person who does not have a weapon. However, just because a criminal has a weapon does not mean that he has to get his way. Many times, the weapon is not intended to kill or injure, but to intimidate. As long as the punk isn't using it, you have the room to move.

Still, there is no guarantee that, even if the knife or gun is a distance from you, your life will be spared. Remember not to listen to promises. Be committed to finding a way out of the situation, but *be careful.*

If a rapist is holding a knife to your throat, you cannot startle him with a sudden move. You have to be more subtle and wait for the right moment to swing into action. Play along with him. Tell him that you'll give him what he wants. Put your arms around his neck and ask him to take the weapon away from your throat. Pull yourself into him slowly, like you want to get closer to him. He'll think that you are seeking comfort from your fear or that you genuinely like him.

Once you are in the right position, find his jugular vein. The jugular veins run on each side of the neck, returning blood from the head to the heart. If you pinch below your jawbone, you can feel it pulsing, parallel to your neck muscle. When a man is excited or tense, his jugulars bulge. If you've no alternative at this point you can sink your teeth deep into his jugular and bite hard.

This maneuver might kill your attacker. It's a drastic measure, but it might be the only choice you have.

It's your life or his.

7

STREET
SMARTS

If you are taking crime-stopping advice from McGruff the cartoon dog, you are in big trouble.

In case you've missed him, McGruff is a trenchcoat-wearing hound seen on public service ads—although the advice he gives is a definite disservice. He recommends removing jewelry before leaving your home or office, and distributing valuables throughout your person so a criminal won't find everything in one spot. But McGruff's real message is: live in fear. His creators apparently believe that the criminals rule the streets and you should tailor your life with this understanding in order to survive. The philosophy enforces the common criminal belief that women are incapable of defending themselves. In the case of hiding one's jewelry, McGruff is joining those countless others who blame the victim; if you're wearing your watch or wedding ring, he is saying, you are tempting the criminal and thus asking to be mugged.

The way you look—your hair, skin color and style of clothing—do not make you a victim. Women are frequent criminal targets because, after a lifetime of being inundated with McGruff-type "advice," they're scared and it shows.

The fact that thugs expect you not to fight back can be used gainfully; you have the element of surprise on your side. Knowing this, and being prepared for specific street encounters, gives you an edge over criminals.

jogging

Many female joggers say "Who would want to attack me?" noting that they carry few valuables when they run, and the paths are usually in bucolic settings. Well, it doesn't matter how scenic—or expensive—the trail; a multimillion-dollar bicycle path in Sacramento, California, has been the site of numerous muggings and at least one murder. Plus, the female jogger entices the rapist's animal drive. Many felons have described watching a woman run as a call to the wild: the first step toward reenactment of the hunt.

Before you run, tell a friend the time you intend to leave and the route. Carry I.D. and change for emergency phone calls. Although you should not put all your faith in a whistle, it is a means of drawing attention to yourself in the event of an assault. Choose a coach's whistle over the dime-store variety.

Leave your personal stereo at home. It destroys your ability to detect footsteps, voices and rustling bushes. When your perception is dulled, a mugger can successfully pounce. For the same reason, avoid wearing a personal stereo in the street.

Make your starting point the least familiar, least populated or most poorly lit part of the trail. You are freshest at the beginning of your run and more capable of accelerating and dodging a mugger.

Stay away from isolated areas and trails passing large clumps of shrubbery in which muggers can hide.

Never assume that you can avoid hoodlums by jogging early. Punks do not keep banker's hours.

Vary your running pattern. A mugger or rapist may be as cognizant of the time the woman in pink shorts passes the park fountain as he is of half-price drinking hours at his local tavern. By changing your routine and/or schedule regularly, no one will know where to lie in wait for you.

In several cities there are services designed to create safe jogging environments for women. In the Washington, D.C., area, Washington Runhers Unlimited published a list of safety tips, as a result of a poll of 128 women in which more than half said they were threatened while jogging. Runhers Unlimited also "matches" females with running partners. In Eugene, Oregon, Project Safe Run, started by a rape victim, rents Doberman dogs for running with women for twenty-five dollars a month.

pay phones

When making a call from a pay phone, do not place your purse between your ankles or on the ledge beneath the telephone. Keep your bag on your shoulder or wrist. If the cord is long enough, stand

DO

DON'T

with your back to the phone, facing any potential danger. With a shorter cord, stand sideways, frequently scanning the street.

bank machines

Although cash machines are convenient, they can be dangerous. Criminals know that the reason most people use them is to withdraw cash; deposits usually wait until the bank opens.

At an outdoor machine, turn around 180 degrees, before inserting your card, to announce to any lurking criminals that you are alert. Stand at a 45-degree angle to the machine when using it, glancing in both directions. Put your money away quickly; counting it will distract you from activity in the street. Before walking away, do another 180-degree turn. Because bank machines may attract unsavory spectators, try to walk away through a crowded street.

If you are using a machine in a glass-enclosed vestibule, make a 180-degree turn, before entering, to check for followers. Stand at a 45-degree angle to the door when unlocking it; if your back is to the street, someone can sneak up behind you and press you against the door. Pull the door shut behind you; do not wait for it to close by itself. Do not admit anyone wishing to enter the vestibule; if he or she has a card, admission will not be a problem. If that person is offended—too bad. Your safety must be your primary consideration. Do not leave the vestibule until you've placed the money in your wallet or purse.

strange neighborhoods

It happens often. You are looking for an address in a newly rebuilt neighborhood but end up in one of the seediest sections of the city. You panic, asking anyone you encounter, "How do I get out of here?" And criminals, sniffing out the fear, strike.

Instead, look for someone in uniform—a cop or mail deliverer—or a gas station attendant to ask directions. Act as if you own the street; like you've been there a million times before. If you are overdressed,

DO

DON'T

the locals may think that you are the owner of one of the buildings—as opposed to a rich person out of her element.

walk in the middle

No matter where you are, walk in the middle of the sidewalk or street. Creeps habitually hide in doorways and alleys, waiting to jump women ambling by. Aside from being far from a mugger's grasp, a female striding down the center of the street appears comfortable; whatever fear she feels is not evident.

being surrounded

So many self-defense books include photos of a woman ringed by attackers and administering martial arts maneuvers to them. In reality, being surrounded by a group of hoodlums is one of the most difficult predicaments to escape. Once they encircle you, they often have a plan in mind. Even advanced martial arts training will bring you only limited success.

Usually, you are not instantly surrounded. One or two thugs try to stop you first. It is crucial that you do not allow yourself to be halted by strangers who ask for a match or the time. When passing a street altercation, do not stop to rubberneck.

If you are encircled, try to use the element of surprise to aid in your escape; throw your grocery bags into the air and move past the thugs who jump to catch them. Never concede defeat; no matter how far outnumbered you are, look for an opening and vow to survive. That is what I did when the three men I told you about in chapter one attacked me, and I think that is why I am alive today.

No one can know every trick in the criminal trade. But by being dedicated to finding a way to stay calm and outlast an encounter, you are that much better off than the millions of people who would allow themselves to be victimized.

8

SUBURBAN SURVIVAL

There are many people who think that an address in the suburbs guarantees safety from the terrors of the inner city, that their most serious concerns should be crabgrass and property values. This misconception lasts only until they find themselves victimized. While no sane person would argue that crime in the suburbs is as widespread as it is in our cities, the fact is that suburban crime is increasing. What's worse is that there is a false sense of security because everyone and everything is spread out, and suburbanites are not subject to the visual threats and intimidation tactics prevalent in densely populated urban jungles.

We like to think that in the suburbs the trouble and the trouble-makers come from the city, whichever city that happens to be. This is an escape fantasy that was a reality in our parents' generation. When they left the city, they left behind crime and other problems for a tranquil and better life. Today, however, we cannot flee crime by moving farther down the commuter line or expressway. Now, there is no complete escape from violence; there is no place left to run and hide. We must face crime, and learn to deal with it as safely and effectively as possible.

who is the suburban criminal?

It is ridiculous to assume that every shopping mall thug is an import from the city. The suburbs are an expensive commute for an urban criminal, and unfamiliar territory. In reality, what's the point of his commuting? There is plenty of action where he lives, plenty of wealth, plenty of goodies to take and very little chance of getting caught. No, the suburban criminal blends in with the environment; he or she reflects the racial and ethnic composition of the area. The suburban criminal looks like anyone's teenage son or daughter, husband or wife, in some cases mother or father.

In the city, the criminal life-support system is found on the streets and in public parks, which are virtually complete miniature models of the American economy. There are wholesalers and distributors of stolen goods, marketing researchers in the form of lowlifes who hang out in doorways and sell tips about who to rip off, even industry watchdogs who help spot the authorities and other hoodlums trying to muscle in on the market share.

In the suburbs, the criminal life-support system is less visible. It thrives on the many service industries that flourish in affluent areas and on the basic trust residents feel for others who can afford to live in the community. The network can include service employees who innocently or intentionally collect information about you, your life-style and possessions: the woman who washes your hair in the beauty salon and overhears you telling a friend about some expensive furnishings you just bought; the gas station attendant who fills up your tank on Friday night and casually inquires about your weekend plans; even your next-door neighbor's son, the one who mows your lawn and knows the layout of your house and the details of your schedule as well as his own.

While the city criminal steals as a full-time occupation for what he or she considers "survival and the necessities," the suburban criminal does it for kicks or to augment legitimate income in order to measure up economically to others in the town. The mecca for street-style crimes—purse snatchings, muggings, sexual assaults— is the site that has become the symbol of American suburbia, the place where women can always be found: the shopping mall.

about shopping malls

One of the most common suburban activities, driving to and from the mall, is fraught with potential danger. Malls seem to be safe places. They have well-lit concourses, crowds and security guards. But step outside a mall, into the parking lot, and you are in no-man's-land.

Often, malls are located in isolated, sparsely populated areas near highways or major commercial thoroughfares. No matter how exclusive the stores are, no matter how modern the facilities and architecture, the lighting in the parking lot is frequently inadequate. In some places, it is nonexistent. This makes the parking lot a mugger's, rapist's and psycho's ideal playground.

A shopping mall was headquarters for a nut who abducted several women in Morris County, New Jersey, in late 1983. Some were murdered. What made it so easy—and what makes malls phenomenally attractive to these vultures—is that a disproportionately large number of women are drawn to them. A woman will frequently go to a mall alone. Working mothers go shopping in the evening while their husbands stay home with the kids. Female shoppers have credit cards. They have cash. They have jewelry, or at least a decent watch or wedding ring. They are very appealing targets.

parking the car

When you park your car, try to get a spot as close to the mall entrance as possible, in the most well-lit section. If you must park at a distance from the entrance, at least try to find a space underneath a light.

To protect your car while you are shopping, don't leave your toll change on the dashboard. Those coins may whet someone's appetite. You may say, "Oh, who's gonna break into my car for seventy-five cents?" But it may start someone thinking, "If there are quarters on the dashboard, maybe there are dollars in the glove compartment." Anything you leave on the seats—even a cheap sweater or jacket—is bait. Loose tape cassettes—it doesn't matter if you paid $2.99 each for them—can provide enough of a temptation to break into your car. It takes nothing for a criminal to smash your windshield or jimmy open the door, and ransack your vehicle. *He* doesn't have to pay for whatever damage he causes.

When you walk from your car to the store, past those rows and rows of autos, walk in the center of the traffic lane. Walking at the edge of the lane, next to the cars, makes you look as if you're cowering. It's not much different from walking in the city. Stride down the middle of the street and you appear confident; walking in the shadow of buildings can make you seem scared. Try to exude a sense of authority, even if you're dog-tired.

By walking in the traffic lane—regardless of how much you must zigzag to let the cars go by—you're out of the reach of creeps who hide between autos. And you're far from any who might be sitting in their cars: they may be there waiting for a friend to come out of a store—or they may be waiting for you.

inside the mall

Usually, malls are replete with security guards. Remember, though, that they are not there for your protection, but to make sure that you and other shoppers do not steal the merchandise. So you have to look out for yourself. While you are preoccupied with searching for bargains and items on your list, an in-store thief may be trying to decide if you and your belongings are the best deal. Don't forget: the in-store thief usually looks like just another shopper!

A common type of indoor mall crime occurs in shoe stores and shoe departments. You're sitting down, trying on shoes, surrounded by shopping bags and your handbag. Once you have the shoes on, you want to walk around, see how they feel and look at them in the mirror. You leave your things on the seat, and when you come back, your wallet is gone.

As difficult as it sounds, if you're alone you have to get in the habit of keeping your things with you at all times. It may be a pain to lug around two shopping bags when you're trying out a new pair of shoes. And you might be concerned that someone may take your seat. But would you rather lose your seat or that expensive wedding gift you just bought? Even if your shopping bag is filled with disposable diapers, someone's liable to take it. A major trait of thieves is that they do not want to miss an opportunity. If something is right in front of them, they'll take it now and examine it later.

Another warning about shoe stores: watch your purse while the salesman is tending to you. When you're sitting on the chair, getting fitted, do not put your purse down on the seat next to you. Someone may dip into it quickly or grab it. Keep your handbag on your lap, or behind your ankles—where you can feel it.

Hoodlums often slice open the side of a handbag and remove the wallet. This can be easily done to a woman trying on shoes—even if she is gripping onto the strap of her purse!

Department store bathrooms can also be a lucrative hangout for thieves. Many restrooms have a bench in them where women can put down their bags and relax for a few moments. But while you're sitting down, another woman may be checking you out. She watches you go into the stall, where you place your purse on the door hook or floor. Then she reaches over or under and grabs it while you're indisposed. When you use the ladies' room, keep your purse on the fold-out shelf near the tissue dispenser, or on your arm or shoulder—even if it may be a little awkward.

Dressing rooms are prime crime areas. You try on clothing in the dressing room, then leave your belongings there while you find a mirror or salesgirl. In the meantime, your purse is left unattended. In some of the fancier department stores, there are not even security guards to limit the number of items brought into the changing area; the management doesn't want to insult you by having a uniformed employee say, "Sorry, you can only take in two things." So you feel very safe and pampered—as if the store couldn't exist without your coming in and dropping a couple of hundred dollars—but it's a false sense of security. While you're posing in front of the three-way mirror, your purse is likely to be stolen.

You have to keep your bag with you at all times. If you want to see how your outfit looks in the mirror without the bag, hold it away from you—so it isn't reflected. Or simply place your purse sideways between your ankles.

Some women put their wallets in their coats, and then leave their coats behind in the dressing room. I'm not advising you to drag your coat around the store with you. But if you leave the dressing room, make sure your wallet is in your hand.

The purse snatcher you find in a women's clothing store is not a burly, unshaven punk with a boom box on his shoulder; the thief is probably another woman. Once, a group of Guardian Angels was standing right outside the entrance of one ritzy department store when a young woman came out of the store screaming, "That lady stole my purse!" Another woman had breezed by her near the exit and grabbed her handbag. The thief was a white, middle-aged woman in a tailored beige raincoat and "sensible" shoes. She could have been anyone's mother. We chased her, caught her and held her for police.

She was protesting, "I didn't take anyone's purse! I didn't take anyone's purse!" But the victim was right there, describing every item in the handbag. After the police arrived, we learned that this innocent-looking perpetrator had *twenty-seven* prior arrests for purse snatching. Naturally, she never spent a great deal of time in prison. Purse snatching is a petty crime. Because of the woman's age and the way she looked, judges were hesitant to throw her in jail with murderers, prostitutes and junkies. I'm sure she realized that her "hobby" was a low-risk crime; that she'd be out and back in the mall quickly. And I'd also bet that for every time she was caught, she committed at least ten successful robberies. Think about it. If your purse was suddenly taken from you, and you were scanning the department store to find the thief, your eyes would probably skip right past this woman.

The area around a department store display case is a bonanza for thieves. Your attention is distracted, as you squint to figure out prices and marvel at the intricacies of the enclosed merchandise. Usually you are carrying either your purse or a shoulder bag. Your purse is under your arm, and the tag of the zipper is jutting out behind you. In a crowded situation, it is not difficult for a practiced pickpocket to casually stroll up behind you, unzip the bag a bit and take out your wallet. Turn the purse or bag around, and get used to having the bulk of it in front of you. Most purse snatchers are gentle and delicate when they work, and don't want to attract attention by reaching into your line of vision to get your goods.

The final ritual of a day of department store shopping—paying the cashier—requires a lot of caution. You put down your bag, take out your wallet, and remove cash, credit cards or a checkbook. But when you're signing a check or sales slip, are you touching your wallet? You should be. Too many women absentmindedly place their wallets on the counter. When they're finished paying the cashier, they are horrified to discover that their wallets are missing.

Destroy your credit card carbons. Discarded carbons can supply a thief with your address and credit card number—which he will use to charge thousands of dollars' worth of purchases to you. A sophisticated criminal may have access to a computer and be able to find out a great deal of information about you by calling up your credit card
number.

parking lot tactics

Now, you're in the parking lot again. Some stores have attendants to help load bags into your car. If you're not at one of these stores or if you choose to carry your own bags, remember to walk in the traffic lane, away from the parked cars. You are more of a vulnerable target now than when you were entering the mall because your hands are full. If someone attacks you from behind, the normal response is, "Oh, my God. I have heavy groceries in my hands. What can I do?" Use your bags as self-defense. Cup your hands underneath your bags, then bring your arms upward and propel the whole load over your head and behind you. Whatever you have in those bags can't be worth more than your life. The mugger's natural reaction is to catch the bags. If he doesn't try catching them, he's going to try sidestepping out of fear of having whatever is in those bags—cans, glass and so on—falling on him. The mugger's distraction buys you time. Run back to the store. If you're in a remote section of the parking lot, run to your car. Or if you're confident, you can use one of the disabling techniques discussed in chapter six.

Get into the habit of putting your purchases into the trunk as soon as you get back to your car. If you will be driving from one group of stores to another, locking your bags up after you finish shopping at one place means you won't have to go through the ritual of removing them from the car at the next location, walking back to the trunk, unlocking it and arousing someone's curiosity.

Before opening your trunk, put your bags down on the car and make a 180-degree turn. That way, if there *is* somebody hiding nearby, he is going to be frightened that you heard him, or you know he's there. A thief knows that a woman who has been shopping is often hungry, thirsty, tired and wants to go home. Making that 180-degree turn tells a potential attacker that you are still alert.

Before you enter your vehicle, look through the window to make sure no one is hiding in the back seat. Also, check the ground around the car; a lot of thugs hide underneath an auto, grab a woman's ankles, knock her down, take her property or rape her—safely hidden between parked cars.

When you unlock the door, keep your feet firmly on the ground, away from the car; if someone underneath grabs you, you won't be knocked totally off-balance.

Leaving breathing room between yourself and the car aids in fending off a criminal who might come up behind you as you're unlocking the door and try to slam you against the auto. His intent, of course, is to force you to the ground. Don't do his work for him. If you leave some space between yourself and the car, and approach the door at a 45-degree angle, he's going to have to exert more energy to get you into the position he wants.

No matter how careful you are, there is always the possibility that—in the case of a small woman, a strong attacker or the suddenness of an assault—you will find yourself pressed against your vehicle, a mugger's forearm over your throat, his other hand grabbing your jewelry, bag or breast. To protect yourself, turn your head to the left or right, in the direction that relieves the pressure on your throat. Now at least you can breathe.

You are still at a disadvantage because your back is turned to your attacker. But, since his body is so close to yours, you have the advantage of being able to feel where all his limbs are. Use your heel to stomp hard on the instep of his foot. Don't aim for his toes; they're too easy to miss. They're the booby prize if you don't get the instep. And if you are right on the mark, it takes five to seven pounds of pressure to collapse the instep bone.

As soon as you damage his foot, go after the arm that's around your neck. Open your mouth as wide as it'll go, and bite his hand. He may not take his arm away, but he will definitely release the pressure.

Spin around. Use the keys in your hand as a weapon. Slash at his face. Wherever you strike, it's going to hurt. Aim for his eyes, though.

Next, jab him in the groin. Now, we were all taught as girls that if a guy gets nasty with you, a swift kick in the family jewels will do the trick. Not necessarily. As mentioned in chapter six, a *knee* in the groin is a lot more effective. When you pull your leg back in order to kick, you run the risk of throwing yourself off-balance—especially if you're wearing a skirt and heels. Grab your attacker by the shoulders to gain momentum while jabbing his groin, and when he bends over in pain, push him—by the shoulders—away from you. Then get away

96

as fast as you can. Hit and run, and remember that once you decide to fight back, it must be a total commitment.

I know a lot of women think, "I can't hurt a guy like that." Why not? What gives anyone the right to come up and attack you? What did you ever do to him to deserve being physically assaulted? Nothing! These guys are mutants. They should be hurt! As soon as a guy lays his hands on you, it's no holds barred.

Again, trusting him not to hurt you if you don't resist is the same as trusting a compulsive gambler who says, "I'm going to quit betting after the eighth race."

We have to psych ourselves to the point where we are willing to do any kind of damage to an attacker. Just because you're in a shopping mall parking lot in a suburb doesn't make your attacker any tamer than an inner-city mugger. Treat him like the animal that he is.

You don't have to be a sadist to fight back. I'm not advocating seriously injuring your attacker. What I am talking about is giving him enough pain that his attention is distracted and you have a chance to flee to safety.

on the road

Even after you are in your car, you still can become the victim of a purse snatcher. A gang of kids in Boston made quite a bit of money by reaching into cars at stoplights and nabbing pocketbooks. A woman in this situation is particularly helpless. She can't just park, leave the car and chase the thief. Take precautions beforehand. Keep the doors locked—even during the daytime when people tend to be more casual. And keep the windows up high enough to prevent a person from reaching in. If it's hot, keep only the window closest to you open; a thief probably won't want to be bothered with reaching across you to get your handbag on the passenger seat or the floor.

If you are driving late at night, and you need gasoline, part with a few extra cents to have an attendant fill up the car for you. Bending over and filling your car with gas at a desolate place makes you too vulnerable—and too visible. A lot of these service stations are located on the edge of the woods or on otherwise isolated commercial   97 strips. If you can't afford the extra money for a full tank, then get a gallon or two and fill up the next day.

A common ruse used by criminals on the road is the fender bender. You're driving down a street, a car comes up behind you and bumps your fender. We've all been taught that your response should be to pull over, get out and exchange licenses, registrations and insurance cards. This may not be wise for a woman traveling alone. Recently, a nun was taking an exit ramp off Route 80, near Paterson, New Jersey, when another car bumped her from behind. She drove onto the shoulder of the road and left her vehicle to meet the other driver, who dragged her into the bushes and raped her.

What should you do if you are driving alone and somebody else bumps your car? Ignore it and keep on going. The bumpers on many late-model cars can take impact of up to twenty-five miles per hour anyway. In most states, deductibles are so high that insurance won't cover your dent being hammered out. Don't chance violence for a stupid little dent.

Staying on the road does not guarantee that a maniac won't continue to follow you. If you are driving alone and sense that someone is tailing you, don't think, "Well, I'll just keep driving until I get home. Then I'll run into my house." That's a bad idea. If someone is following you, *don't* show him where you live.

If someone is trailing your car, do a few test moves—just as you would if you suspected you were being followed on the street. Get off at an exit. Make a series of turns. Most important, get to a place where there are other people. Go to a service station where there are attendants, a motel you know is open twenty-four hours a day or an all-night diner. If you want to track down a cop, drive to the closest twenty-four-hour doughnut stand. You can always find the police at doughnut stands.

Police might be able to save you from an individual crime threat, but each concerned citizen must work to save the suburbs. If law-abiding folks are committed to fighting crime, the plague that has ravaged bedroom communities can be stopped.

9

ON THE GO: TROUBLE IN TRANSIT

If someone came up to me in any city and asked, "Where can I find some crime around here?" I'd recommend the bus or train station. Anybody can gain admittance to a terminal, and thus creeps tend to congregate there. Besides providing shelter from inclement weather, a depot is often packed with travelers carrying cash, credit cards, jewelry, clothing and gifts; a criminal would be hard-pressed to find a better place to ply his or her trade.

entering the station

When you purchase your ticket or token, ask about the schedule and gate location. If you question other commuters about these subjects, criminals may detect your disorientation. When you know where you're going, you project confidence.

While heading for the gate, be wary of anyone asking for directions, the time or a match. He may be trying to stop you as a preliminary to mugging. Tell him you are in a hurry and continue walking.

Do not hand your bag to anyone not in uniform. Stations are popular hangouts for vultures who offer to carry your luggage, or find you a cab and/or hotel room. It is common for a tourist, tired, confused and possibly taken aback by a terminal's seedy appearance, to fall victim to this ploy. At the very least, the parasite is checking you out to determine robbery potential. Do you have an accent? Are you overwhelmed by a new city? Do you have a ride waiting for you? What are you carrying?

Sometimes, your "helper" will carry your bag to the street, then agree to return it—for a ten-dollar fee. More often, he'll simply run with your belongings. If a cohort is not waiting for him in a nearby car, he can easily lose you by hopping onto a local train or bus. He knows the city. You don't.

I know of one woman who had her bag stolen this way. She wandered into the street, only to have the thief's partner mug her.

one bag is best

The best way to avoid this problem is to take along just one piece of baggage. A large nylon bag with a shoulder strap is excellent; even when it's very full, you can still carry it yourself and not seem weighed down. A mugger will probably pass you by for someone struggling with her luggage.

Even when commuting locally, it is best to place all shopping items in one large bag. In case of trouble, you have one free hand and can swing or push your bag into an assailant.

Of course, you will not always be able to fit everything in one bag. It might be better, however, to pay shipping costs than be burdened with excess luggage on a trip.

stay with your stuff

Try to take your bag everywhere you go in the terminal. Some commuters see a pleasant-looking person and ask, "Can you please watch my things while I go to the ladies' room?" However, even if the person's intentions are honest, there is no guarantee that your property will remain where you left it. Your watcher may abandon your bag upon learning that his bus is leaving. Even a clerk or uniformed worker watching your bag in the bus or train company office can be called to another part of the terminal for an emergency.

panhandling versus mugging

Panhandlers are a fact of bus and train station life. They should not intimidate you—if you can distinguish between them and muggers.

A panhandler is passive. He stands against a wall or posts himself in one spot like a fixture. Although he may beg, *he does not demand.*

You should be less fearful of him than those watching you give him money. When you stop, put your belongings down and fish through your purse to perform your good deed, some leech may steal your bag. It is more practical to keep loose change in a side pocket and give charity without breaking stride, if you feel so inclined.

When someone aggressively asks for money, he is not panhandling—he is setting you up to be mugged. If, frightened, you stop and comply, he—and possibly several accomplices—will clean you out.

Without halting, answer the depot extorter with a stern no. Be as vocal as possible to attract attention: "Give *you* five dollars? Are you crazy? Do you think I'm made out of money?" Most likely, he'll conclude that you're too much trouble to pursue.

It shouldn't matter how sad this person looks. Remember: his sympathies do not go out to you.

airports

At one time, airports did not attract the same type of criminals as train and bus terminals. This has changed. Mass-transit systems in many cities—such as New York, Chicago and San Antonio—now run directly to airports. An inner-city punk has only to invest in a cheap fare or hop a turnstile to be provided with hundreds of "suckers," many of whom do not speak English. There are sophisticated rings of well-dressed, jet-set thugs who prey upon successful-looking business travelers. A fresh crop of victims has also sprung up in recent years due to discounted air fares. Take the same precautions in airports that you would in train and bus stations.

platforms

On train platforms, stand closest to the nearest attendant, ticket window or token booth. This might mean waiting at the top of a flight of stairs and then running quickly down when you hear your train arriving. An alternative is staying in a well-lit area. You may feel more conspicuous there, but you are a less attractive victim if others can *see* a mugger assault you.

103

bus shelters

Bus shelters were designed to provide relief from the weather. Unfortunately, they've become muggers' alcoves. Many are made of tinted glass and are covered with advertisements, thereby providing a concealed and isolated stronghold for criminal activity. When waiting for the bus alone, stay outside the shelter, where you can view the surrounding area and where a hood cannot corner you.

boarding psychology

Most people feel less powerful on a bus or train than they do in the street; they are confined; someone else is driving and operating the doors. Be conscious of this, and do not allow your sense of strength to be stripped when you board. Realize that by trusting your instincts, a way can be found out of *every* situation.

finding a seat

The ideal seat for a passenger—near the doors—is also the mugger's hotseat. Within seconds, he can grab your chain, purse or briefcase, cut through the closing doors and disappear. And don't expect the bus driver or conductor—under pressure to follow schedules—to stop so you can chase the thief. By taking a seat farther from the exit, you are decreasing your chances of being robbed.

The back of the bus or train is usually the party center for troublemakers, who congregate there drinking, smoking reefers, blasting their boom boxes and shouting. If you sit close to the driver, you are less likely to find yourself surrounded by punks.

subway windows

On subways, avoid sitting next to open windows. Many muggers stand in stations, reach through the windows of departing trains and grab chains and earrings.

reading

Because a rapid-transit ride is hardly exhilarating, many read to pass the time. However, even when you are skimming through a trashy novel, a mugger can tell that your full concentration is not on protecting your belongings.

avoiding thugs

On the subway, if you feel someone is checking you out, move to another car. Some women are reluctant to do this because they do not want the guys watching them to know they're afraid. However, if you are trembling in your seat, your feelings are obvious. Moving is viewed as a decisive action, an announcement that you do not wish to be a victim. It is equivalent to crossing the street to avoid passing a group of hoodlums.

On the bus, it might be harder to get away from a band of criminals. Rather than sitting, petrified, for an entire trip, leave and wait for the next bus. Even if you are late for an appointment, you will have avoided the possibility of being victimized.

rush hour

Rush hour commuting is not as safe as it seems. You cannot relax your guard because the bus or train is crowded with men in tan topcoats and women in business suits. Muggers, aware of the pervading sense of security, wait for rush hour to employ certain techniques: pickpocketing and slicing open purses, coat pockets and pants pockets with razors.

Those few moments when you are squeezing on and off the vehicle is the perfect time for a thief to strike. It is easy to forget, as you push and shove to find a seat or exit, where your belongings are. The most important principle for rush hour commuters should be: watch your valuables closely.

jostlers

Rush hour is also attractive to jostlers, perverts who derive pleasure from grabbing or rubbing against a woman in a crowd. These creeps depend upon the deplorable female traditions of passivity and self-victimization to get their jollies. The victims often feel shamed by a jostling episode, while their molesters go away unreprimanded and undetected. It is up to you to shift the blame to where it belongs. When someone purposely brushes against you, scream, "Get your *filthy* hands off me!" Point at him so the other passengers will know the target of your anger. Chances are that the jerk will bolt through the doors as soon as they open.

distraction techniques

A fabricated disturbance is a criminal technique that can fool even the very street wise. A loud argument or shoving match breaks out on a moving train or bus. The noninvolved passengers, bored and wishing they could arrive at their destinations sooner, welcome the departure from tedium. Meanwhile, a cohort of the arguers is casually lifting valuables from the rapt passengers. He or she exits before anyone realizes a crime has occurred. Although it may be tempting, avoid allowing yourself to become absorbed in an in-transit altercation.

real altercations

Of course, not every argument is staged. Usually loud scenes involve little more than people blowing off steam. Follow the same rule as the Guardian Angels: if it's verbal, ignore it.

You should worry when the combatants move into your personal space. Get away; don't expect other passengers to aid you if stray blows fly your way. On a train, move into another car. On a bus, where you have less maneuverability, it might be practical to exit and wait for the next ride.

followers

For some reason, followers—men who trail women like shadows—consider trains and terminals attractive starting points. Being followed isn't dangerous. Having your follower catch you in some deserted location *is.* Your safety depends on your remaining calm and evaluating your options.

There are three types of followers:

The first type is mentally disturbed. He may be a former mental patient and heavily medicated. His motive for latching on to you is unclear. If you are not nervous, you will be able to sense his disorientation and harmlessness. Try to shake him off your trail by switching cars. If he persists in following you, tell him, "Look, I know what you're doing, and if you don't stop, I'm gonna mess you up." However, his illness may prevent him from understanding. When I have been in this predicament, I realized that this type of follower would not hurt me, and I tried to disregard him as I continued to my destination.

The second type is a criminal scoping you out. He may be working with a partner or group. Treat him as you would a threatening pack of guys on the street. Do not reveal your fear, but convey your knowledge of and disgust with the situation by changing cars. If the follower pursues you, move again . . . and again. Many thugs do not want to run after someone hip to their act when other targets are so close by. Try to settle in a populated section of the train. When the follower approaches, announce, "This jerk has been following me everywhere!" building empathy among the other passengers.

An even better ploy is to find the conductor or bus driver and complain to him. He can radio for help, if necessary. However, conductors are difficult to locate. Many, terrified of being victimized themselves, lock themselves in their booths. Likewise, bus drivers, often justifiably, are more afraid for their own safety than for yours.

Pulling the emergency cord is a poor move. The train will halt, and your follower may be able to take advantage of you in the ensuing confusion.

The third type can be called the "habitual follower." He is infatuated with you and knows your regular routine: what time you board, where you sit, where you exit. He may be waiting for you on the train when you enter each day, or follow you to your office. He is obsessed enough to dig deep to learn personal facts about your life. You may be the object of his anger and frustration at not being able to enjoy a healthy relationship. Frequently, this type rapes.

The best way to throw him off-track is by changing your pattern—even if it means waking up a half hour earlier in order to avoid him. Normally, I am not in favor of having you adjust your life to deal with criminals, but here I make an exception.

standing up for yourself while sitting down

The Guardian Angels can always tell which riders do not regularly take the subway: the ones who sit with crossed legs. Anyone accustomed to the spur-of-the-moment calamity of rapid transit wouldn't do that. If an emergency arises, you cannot stand quickly. If someone is menacing you from a standing position, you cannot use your foot for self-defense. Keeping your knees together and feet flat on the ground gives you the dexterity needed when suddenly preyed upon.

There is nothing wrong with a man's sitting next to you and trying to make friends—as long as he keeps his hands to himself. When he touches you—no matter how gently or how friendly his demeanor—consider it assault.

Although an encounter with a criminal on a bus or train is frightening, you can protect yourself by allowing your instincts to direct you toward the proper course of action. Never lose sight of your power, and be prepared to use it.

10

HOME SWEET HOME

A woman's home should be her castle. Criminals, however, view a single woman, living alone or with children, as a perfect target. Your vulnerability increases when your living status can be easily determined. The first step in home security is keeping your life-style a mystery from strangers.

the vaguer, the better

The easiest way to track down a woman is through the telephone directory. A criminal who looks over your shoulder in a store and learns your name from a check or credit card slip only has to pick up the phone book to discover your address. This can be avoided, without getting an unlisted number. In many places, you can have your name and telephone number listed without your address. Another option is keeping your number on file with directory assistance, but not in the phone book. Ask the telephone company to catalog you under your first initial, rather than your full first name. While potential dates, business contacts and friends will be able to call you, criminals will be unable to find out where you live.

As I have pointed out in the chapter on suburban survival, you must edit your conversations in public places. The mention in a shop of an upcoming trip can be transformed into a hot lead on the local crime circuit. For instance, you tell your friend at the beauty parlor, "I'm getting my hair frosted for the convention next week in Butte, Montana." The stylist, coffee delivery man and another customer are within earshot. You don't know who is listening—and who may pass this information on or use it in the plotting of a burglary.

When you travel, be wary of taxi and limousine drivers who take you to the airport. There may be a sinister motive behind their seemingly harmless questions about your home furnishings and travel agenda. Do not allow a driver to identify you by a particular apartment or doorbell. If you live in an apartment building, wait for your 111 ride in the lobby. If you live in a house, wait on the corner. Although the driver will know your block, he will be unable to detect where you live on it.

know your apartment building

Before moving into an apartment building, familiarize yourself with it. Know all the entrances and exits. Make sure that fire exits can be opened only from the inside. Side doors should not be randomly left open. Acquaint yourself with every access. Even in buildings with doormen and elaborate intercom systems, there are service entrances that few people know about, except criminals. Many times these are left open for the convenience of deliverymen.

If your building does not have a doorman, make sure the front door locks behind you. In most states, there are laws requiring landlords to repair broken front locks. It is up to the tenants to ensure that those laws are followed.

The hallways and stairways must be well lit, in order to deter attackers who hide behind steps, garbage cans, furniture and corners. Blind spots should be reflected in mirrors, like the ones in stores that aid in preventing thefts. Don't feel bashful about asking your landlord to install mirrors; it is better to seem like a nuisance than to be mugged. If your landlord does not install mirrors, join other tenants in pressuring him. If he still does not meet your demands—and there are no legal actions you can take against him—put up the mirrors yourselves. In a large building, a dollar a person can buy a mirror for every stairwell. And when tenants organize, the word goes out among the neighborhood criminals that your building is the wrong one to hit.

laundry and compactor rooms

The laundry and compactor rooms, with their noise and isolation from the rest of the building, are prime spots for criminals. If these rooms have one doorway, enter them only in the company of a friend.

Even then, do not go to the laundry or compactor room during an off-hour. Cleanliness is a virtue, except when attaining it endangers your life.

You are particularly vulnerable in the laundry room, where criminals know there is always a handy selection of females. Keep your laundry basket, clothes bag or shopping cart *in front of you* when you enter, to act as a shield from potential attackers. A box of soap powder or container of detergent can be used as part of your self-defense arsenal. Tossing a cleaning substance at a laundry room vulture will blind him and buy you the seconds you need to run to safety.

protecting your house

Aside from having a vicious attack dog, one of the best ways to protect your house from burglars is by installing outdoor lighting. The more lights there are, the safer you will feel, and the more uncomfortable a criminal will be. If he has a question about robbing your home or another on the block, he is definitely going to choose the house where the lighting is less adequate and his chance of being spotted is less likely.

Flood the outside of your house with light. From the front door to the back porch, every access should be illuminated. I know that many people say, "I don't want a well-lit doorway. Criminals will be able to see me come and go." But think of how the criminal feels. If he can see you entering and leaving, you—and your neighbors—can also see him.

While apartment building criminals hide behind stairwells, housebreakers use trees and shrubs for camouflage. This is why it's important to bathe your lawn and garden with light. Your electric bills will go up, but you and your possessions will be safer.

Your garage should be equipped with manual or automatic lights that illuminate the outside and inside when you are parking. A gravel driveway can further secure the area. The sound of footsteps or tires on gravel will alert you and your neighbors to criminal activity in the driveway or garage.

the rural home

Even though lighting may be somewhat of a crime deterrent in rural areas, I know that if I lived in a farm house—thirty or forty miles from the nearest police station—I'd have a shotgun. When your screams cannot be heard by neighbors, a shotgun blast will definitely get your message across.

Urbanites reading this may think, "But what if you have children? It is not safe to keep guns around kids." This is true to a point. But people I know in rural areas do not treat firearm safety lightly. They give their children early gun training. The youngsters learn not only how to handle guns, but to respect them. In the country, guns are a way of life, not a last resort for desperate people.

If you choose to keep a gun in your house, you'd better know it intimately. Guns in the hands of untrained people often spell disaster. The last thing you want is a criminal taking your weapon from your hands and using it on you.

security

I am not a big fan of the "popular" security systems. Window bars, metallic tape, locks and stickers broadcasting how your premises are protected may look intriguing, but they can actually entice burglars. Many criminals examine doors and windows and conclude, "Man, this person spent a hundred dollars on that one lock alone. Imagine how much she must have spent on the things inside her home."

People do not take burglar alarms seriously. Have you ever heard an alarm go off as you were walking down the street? Did you call the police? Most people do not. They think, "Ah, a cat or the rain set it off." Rarely do they believe that a home or car is being burglarized.

Certain burglar alarms are wired to private security companies that are supposed to send someone to investigate. But consider who these guys are: untrained security guards who frequently can find no other job. Some are ex-cons. They are usually paid minimum wage and are not going to risk their lives to protect the property of someone whose monthly rent is equivalent to their annual income. There have been cases of security guards selling tips on the homes they watch to help supplement their meager salaries without getting their hands dirty.

Even those security systems wired to police stations do not guarantee that a crime in your home will be thwarted. From my experience with the Guardian Angels, I've learned that the police, on the average, respond to this type of call approximately one hour and fifteen minutes after they receive it.

The ultimate alarm system is one that contacts not the police or badge-carrying "protectors," but neighbors. A burglar alarm system can easily be wired between your home and others nearby. The more people on the system, the better. When your alarm goes off, one neighbor calls the police while the others converge on your home, shining lights, making noise, intimidating the criminal. Once word gets out that this is the way your neighborhood reacts to crimes, thieves will bypass your area for those with less diligent and aggressive inhabitants.

When a neighborhood decides to band together, punks don't have a chance. In the summer of 1985, Los Angeles was terrorized by a "night stalker" who entered homes through unlocked doors and windows, raped the women he found, killed the men and sometimes spray-painted pentagrams on the walls. For over seven months, he allegedly killed fourteen people. The day after a photo of suspect Richard Ramirez appeared on television and in the newspapers, he was spotted in East Los Angeles. A crowd began to pursue him, down streets and through backyards. As word spread throughout the neighborhood, others joined the chase. By the time police became involved, a battered Ramirez must have been grateful for being rescued from the dozens of outraged citizens who had made a choice not to live in fear.

locks

A lot of people use locks to shield themselves from the outside world. However, two locks are as good as eight. The first should be a sturdy key lock, located just below your door knob. This is the one to which your landlord should have the key (if you choose to give it to him; I recommend extreme caution before letting anybody have access to your home). The second should be a deadbolt lock that can be opened, without a key, only from the inside. If someone manages to jimmy open the first lock, you are still protected.

A window lock is pretty useless because a criminal can easily break a small hole in the glass, reach in, undo the lock, lift up the window and climb into your home. It is more effective to drill holes through the top and bottom sashes of the window frame and place a thick nail or screw through each hole. The only alternative this leaves a burglar is removing your entire window, causing a commotion and increasing the chances of being discovered.

guarding your windows

Like other visible security measures, window bars can attract criminals to your home. If you are the only person with window bars in your building, burglars conclude that your possessions are the most valuable. By contrast, if yours is the only apartment *without* window bars, you are equally as vulnerable.

The biggest drawback of window bars is the danger they cause during a fire in your home. In places like New Orleans, where many older houses are made of wood, bars are as much a threat to your safety as the assailant who comes upon you in your sleep. If you live in a neighborhood where you feel it is important to board up your windows, European-style mini-barn doors are better. They are closed from the inside, yet can be opened quickly enough to let you escape a blaze.

If you do not want to seal yourself in, you can place decorative Christmas bells around your windows. There is no way a burglar can pass those bells and crawl into your home without making a great deal of noise. That enables you to phone for help, leave your home or confront the hoodlum.

What I like even more is a trick I learned from my Italian relatives. Put broken glass, nails and jagged metal pieces on your windowsills. Anyone trying to get a grip and boost himself into your home will be forced to endure a great deal of pain. This may get the burglar thinking, "If this person planned so well at the window stage, who knows what awaits me inside?"

Placing sharp objects around your window does not endanger you in the event of a fire. Since, unlike the criminal, you do not have to reach upward to touch your windowsill, you can step over the prickly bits safely.

pretending you're home

Generate the illusion that you are home when you are away.

Make sure mail does not accumulate in front of your door. Have a neighbor pick up your letters, or ask the post office to hold them for you until you return.

In an apartment, leave the television on—a portable set, not a large one that uses a great deal of electricity. Burglars know that apartment dwellers leave radios on to avert crime. But they associate the sound of a television set with an owner sitting in front of it.

Leave lights on—not living room lights, which burglars expect to be on, but bedrom and bathroom lights. It's a good idea to purchase a timer to turn your lights, stereo and television on and off at intervals.

You can scare away the thief who peeks in your window by creating the impression that you are in another room. Spread out a newspaper on the floor, as if it's being read. Place a half-filled bowl of popcorn on the table, with a kernel or two dropped nearby. Leave a lipstick-marked glass of water in sight. Remember: many burglars are cowards and do not want to confront you.

your guests are your choice

Even though it's been said a million times before: check the credentials of anybody who comes to work in your home. If the utility company man or telephone repairman cannot properly identify himself, do not let him in!

When you need something repaired, use a handyman known in the community—even if he is more expensive than someone randomly selected from the Yellow Pages or a roving Mr. Fix-It. Be careful about handymen who place ads. Some view a visit to your home as a chance to figure out what to return to steal.

As cruel as it may sound, you must be tough with people who ring your bell because of what they say is an emergency. Do not let them in to use the phone. Ask them for the number they want called and the message they want conveyed, then make the call for them.

going to your apartment

When entering your building, remove your keys in the lobby, so you can concentrate on self-protection as you make that sometimes perilous journey to your apartment. Lace the keys between your fingers like brass knuckles. Make a 180-degree turn to inform attackers that you're no easy target. Practice this procedure so it comes naturally.

Wait for the elevator standing sideways, a good distance from the doors. This prevents someone from pushing you into the elevator from the rear, or pulling you in with them. As you wait, make the 180-degree turn again.

Before entering the elevator, look inside. If you feel uncomfortable, follow your instincts. Tell the unsavory character inside, "Oh, I forgot something," and let him go up without you.

Move in and out of the elevator with your body turned slightly sideways. This leaves less body surface vulnerable to attack, and you have a better chance of preventing the doors from closing.

Inside, stand with your back to the wall, near the buttons. This way, no one can attack you from behind, and you can reach the emergency bell.

If someone threatening gets on, slip off and wait for another elevator.

Upon exiting, make the 180-degree turn in your corridor. Someone with designs of following you *will* if you look vulnerable.

To expedite things, keep your keys in your right hand if you're right-handed, the left hand if you're left-handed. Approach your door at a 45-degree angle, leaving about twelve inches between your body and the door, so no one can quickly press you against it. Stand sideways in order to be able to look from side to side in a natural way.

Just before you enter your apartment, scan the hall. Never forget that muggers can sneak up behind you very quickly and quietly. In urban areas, they're fond of "push-in crimes"—descending upon someone as she's opening her door and pushing her into the apartment. On the street, we have an expression: "Watch your back." Apply it when you leave the street as well.

Most people are usually so anxious to get into their apartments that they dive through the door. This conveys fear. Slow down. Project confidence. Let the thugs think you own the building. This is your territory, and use your body language to tell everyone you intend to guard it fiercely.

After your door is open, don't dally in front of it. Remove the key, go inside, *close and lock the door behind you* and then put your key away.

coming home to a burglary

If you arrive home to an open door or other signs of a possible break-in, *do not* enter. Go to the nearest phone and call police. Alert neighbors that a burglar may be in the vicinity. If possible, park your car with the high beams focusing on the areas of the break-in. Wait for the police to arrive before entering your home.

the night stalker

Earlier in this chapter, I mentioned a California criminal known as the "night stalker." Just as you would prepare for a fire, you must prepare for this type of mutant who thrives on the fact that his victims are asleep and thus totally vulnerable.

Expect the worst. Picture yourself in bed and imagine that four guys with shotguns have broken into your home. How do you get out of there? It's similar to waking up and smelling smoke. You may not be able to leave through the front door. Know your avenues of flight.

Also, know your capabilities. You're not going to have time to fix yourself a cup of coffee. How will you function seconds after you wake up? If you know you will be slow, overprepare.

The advantage you have is that you know your home better than the intruder. You know the exits, the hiding spots and, if such is your desire, the best places to attack someone.

Some people feel that you have no right to strike an intruder in your home unless he is doing you physical harm. That's garbage. I don't think there's a court in the world that would convict you for disabling a night stalker. When someone is violating your home, that person is violating you. All is fair in that game; he deserves whatever's coming to him.

dual-purpose weapons

Many common items can be used to thwart off an attacker. Keep them in places where you can quickly grab them. There's no need to tell yourself, "Oh, my God, I have these deadly weapons in my house." Just know they're there in case you need them.

A cane is a great weapon. It's light and easy to handle. When using it on an attacker, don't swing at the head. That's what the night stalker expects, and you'll be putting your body in an awkward position. Aim for the legs, the knees and the ankles. Someone who can't walk can't chase you. You'll have the time to either run or attack further.

Another good weapon is a rolling pin. The handle is perfect for jabbing at the head, preferably near the eyes. It doesn't require a great deal of strength to swing, yet it's heavy enough to hurt when it hits.

A can of aerosol spray looks perfectly normal perched on an end table. But when an uninvited guest is rampaging through your home, an inexpensive air freshener can save your life. Use the spray to blind an attacker. Then, follow your instincts to leave or attack further.

Don't forget your grandmother's specialty: the frying pan. One of those cast-iron pans can really do a number on someone's head.

The way I see it, any violence done to an intruder is warranted. A woman's home is her castle, and you must take the attitude that invading armies had better cast their sights on other kingdoms.

11

QUESTIONS AND ANSWERS

In order to truly understand your ability—and responsibility—to defend yourself, certain questions must be answered. In conducting street survival seminars and talking with women throughout the United States and Canada, I've heard numerous queries repeated over and over. Below are the most common, and important, ones:

Q: *What is the most serious emotional problem women have?*
A: The fear of not being liked and loved. Women are trained to please people in order to be appreciated. When a criminal preys on a woman, it is clear that he has no fondness for her. Out of habit, some women are willing to give up their lives and bodies in order to change his feelings; rape victims have told therapists they submitted because they wanted their attackers to like them. This warped and self-destructive world view must be changed. Accept that there are creatures out there who dislike not only you, but people in general. If you are attacked, don't take it personally. Instead of trying to appeal to the creep, hurt him and leave.

Q: *Do you honestly believe that most women can change their attitudes concerning crime, or are you being idealistic?*
A: I am not being idealistic, I'm being practical. Women *can* and *must* change their attitudes about crime. In this generation, we have taken on challenges that our mothers and grandmothers would never have imagined. If other obstacles can be overcome, so can a defeatist perspective concerning crime. Many women have told me that they would battle crime—if they only knew how. Now, you have a start.

Q: *There's an expression, "What you don't know won't hurt you." Will knowing all the ways I can be assaulted actually backfire and increase my fear?*
A: When it comes to crime, what you don't know can kill you. When you know what can occur in this not-always-friendly world, you can be prepared not to become another sad statistic.

A new piece of information makes a person afraid only when she is *already* scared. For too many women, fear is like a migraine headache that never goes away: it emanates from thinking that we are incapable of handling a criminal encounter. In order to be able to walk the streets in confidence, you must examine and be ready for even the most terrifying scenarios.

In time, taking the proper precautions will become second nature to you. When you see a group of threatening guys down the block, you'll automatically cross the street—just as you'd automatically reach for an umbrella if you heard it was going to rain.

Q: How do I best translate my fear into the anger necessary to strike an attacker?

A: As soon as you are attacked, you should pull a trigger inside of you to summon up anger. Because women often see themselves as nurturers, it might be easier to be brave by imagining another person in your place. Think, "What if somebody was doing this to my mother or child?" Once your wrath has been set off, your adrenaline will start pumping and your instincts will lead you in the right direction.

This is how the criminal is able to muster up bravado. He says, "That woman has the same dress on as the one who wouldn't give me a job and the same hairstyle as the one who wouldn't go out with me." He regards his victim as a terrible person who deserves whatever she's going to get; he stokes his anger like a fire. What he doesn't realize is that his psychology can be used against him; you have the chance to give him the surprise of his life!

Q: How can I maintain the right attitude?

A: I don't expect you to remember every physical technique discussed. But choose those that you feel would be easiest to perform—based on your height, age, size and fitness level—and practice them with a friend.

Understand that more important than the physical techniques is knowing that you have the choice to fight back. Know that your key to triumphing over a thug is to remain calm and trust yourself.

Q: How can I learn to trust myself?

A: This society puts too much emphasis on "expert" advice. You are told to trust the beauty expert, legal expert, financial expert and psychological expert. In a subtle and insidious way, the dependency on those "authorities" undermines the trust you should feel for yourself.

When you make a mistake, instead of criticizing yourself, explore why you made the error. You'll be surprised at how many times the answer will be, "I didn't trust my instincts." For example, you get the feeling that the local train will be faster than the express train and, sure enough, the express train stalls that morning. Trusting your intuition—or "gut feeling"—enables you to arrive on time.

Think about how you can avoid repeating mistakes in the future. If you can learn from an error, it ceases to be one.

Q: After learning the techniques discussed, will most women have the courage to jab attackers' eyes with their fingertips?
A: I hope they will. Women should refuse to accept the victim mentality and learn to take action. Of course, I know that many say that biting, scratching and eye-poking is gross. But getting gross for a few minutes is preferable to living with feelings of powerlessness and self-hate for not having resisted an assault.

Q: Is there a danger of being overconfident?
A: I've never seen a woman with the same false macho pride that a man has who learns one punch in karate school and then challenges everyone.

I've never advised anyone to court trouble. My advice is, Cross the street when you see a group of guys that make you feel uncomfortable. Ignore verbal abuse unless you are prepared to battle. If you are physically confronted, however, there is no danger in knowing you can fight back. Having confidence in your ability to counter an attack can save your life.

Q: Will my new attitude detract from my femininity?
A: Absolutely not. The attitude is like your personal, internal guardian angel. It's there when you need it to deal with the unpleasant aspects of the world. Otherwise, it lies in a dormant state. It is not something you carry around like a chip on your shoulder.

You can be strong and feminine at the same time. If you have the right attitude and a familiarity with basic self-defense maneuvers, you can put down a creep without even breaking a fingernail.

Q: Will my relationship with men be affected?

A: Often, a man feels threatened when his wife or girlfriend begins learning self-defense. He may see your training as an indication that he cannot adequately protect you (in reality, no one can guard you twenty-four hours a day). After a while, he will see that you are just as feminine as you were before, and your new knowledge does not make him any less masculine. Then, he will probably feel relief that he doesn't have to worry about you constantly.

Eventually, your training will make your relationship stronger; it will definitely balance it out. My husband considers me his equal in intelligence and ability to defend myself—and no one ever accused Curtis of being a wimp!

When you delve into the origins of your fear, be careful not to unleash your pent-up anger from past injustices on the man closest to you. Likewise, don't get mad at yourself about the past. Just vow to do better in the future.

Q: What are the legal ramifications if I fight back and severely injure my assaulter?

A: You are not violating any laws by injuring someone who has threatened to harm you or take your property. Even if you kill your attacker—and save the taxpayers the burden of feeding and housing him in prison (that is, if the punk should defy the odds by being convicted)—you will not be charged as a criminal in most states. In Detroit, a woman was exonerated after stabbing a rapist forty-seven times. A jury ruled that her action was warranted due to the menacing circumstances.

If you refuse to be a victim and some sick district attorney tries to make a name for himself by railroading you, I promise that the Guardian Angels will come to your aid to demand justice—as we have done for others in the past.

After I was attacked in 1983, I lay in my hospital bed, feeling paranoid, vulnerable and sorry for myself. Here I thought I was Wonder Woman, and now I was a bruised casualty of three goons. Then, I looked at the patients in the other beds. Some were elderly and infirm, others had incurable ailments. I considered myself lucky to be alive and on the road to recovery.

126   Even though I had been beaten up, I was proud that I had been

successful in my refusal to submit to rape. Not only had my attitude saved me, but it made me feel like a survivor.

I realized then that every woman has two options: constant paranoia or using the lessons of self-defense to stand tall. One person *can* make a difference; all revolutions start with an individual.

Before the quality of life can be improved on this planet, people must make an effort to better their own lives. That begins with taking a hard look at yourself and asking, "Is my life worth fighting for?"

I hope you say yes.

acknowledgments

It seems that with any project, no matter how simple, a few people get the credit while many others labor behind the scenes. This book is no different!

It could not have been written without the help of the following interns who worked diligently, productively and under tight deadlines: Willie Diaz, Marie-Therese Hernon, Richard Behrens and Mark Whinston. I also appreciate the last-minute typing assistance provided by Norma Greenberg, my coauthor's mother.

In addition to my street experiences, the ideas in this book are the result of thousands of hours of seminars, workshops, interviews and conversations made possible by dedicated men and women. I would like to thank Don Epstein and the staff of Greater Talent Network, my lecture agency, for arranging the seminars that allowed me to present these concepts to large audiences.

I am indebted to Grace Mirabella, publisher, Dorothy Schefer, Beauty News Editor, and the other editors of *Vogue* for having the guts to be the first women's magazine to deal with the subject of women's self-defense.

Literary agent Geri Thoma should be recognized for her persistence in making this book a reality. Our editor, Barbara Grossman, deserves an award for her determination and guidance. It is no easy feat to work on a book with someone who hates to sit down! No one knows this better than my coauthor, Keith Greenberg, who went way above and beyond the call of duty in helping me communicate my thoughts and meet the deadlines. He expresses his appreciation to his agent, Lisbeth Mark, and to Carmine Bellucci.

I would also like to thank the Guardian Angels who have participated in my street survival seminars and have so willingly volunteered to be thrown around for the sake of education.

$9.95 (Higher in Canada)/PSYCHOLOGY/SELF-DEFENSE

IT'S NOT SURVIVAL OF THE FITTEST... IT'S SURVIVAL OF THE SMARTEST!

If there's one woman who has proved that brains can conquer brawn, it's dynamic Lisa Sliwa, outspoken national director of America's most celebrated public defenders, the Guardian Angels. In *Attitude*, Lisa draws on her years of experience patrolling New York City's meanest streets to provide women (and the men who care about them) with sensible and successful tactics for self-protection. Hers is the first book ever to arm women with the *only* weapons that work: the street smarts to avoid danger and the confidence to escape it.

Illustrated with more than two dozen photographs of Lisa in action, *Attitude* provides a complete range of self-defense strategies: at home, on mass transit, on the street or in a shopping mall, a parking lot or a car. And by exposing and dissecting the psychology of muggers, hoodlums and rapists, *Attitude* aims to help women reject the role of helpless victim and outwit any attacker.

Tough, brainy and beautiful, Lisa Sliwa is *the* role model for every woman who wants to protect herself without becoming a female Dirty Harry. Lisa Sliwa's got an attitude...and it's going to change the way American women live.

CROWN PUBLISHERS, INC., 225 PARK AVENUE SOUTH, NEW YORK, NEW YORK 10003

Cover photo by Bill Bernstein

ISBN 0-517-56187-5